N A T I V E ✳ A M E R I C A N ✳ C U L T U R E

DAILY LIFE

Barbara McCall

Series Editor
Jordan E. Kerber, Ph.D.

✳ ✳ ✳

ROURKE PUBLICATIONS, INC.
Vero Beach, Florida 32964

©1994 by Rourke Publications, Inc.

A Blackbirch Graphics book.

Printed in the United States of America.

Library of Congress Cataloging-in-Publication Data

McCall, Barbara A., 1936–
Daily life / by Barbara McCall.
     p. cm. — (Native American culture)
     Includes bibliographical references and index.
     ISBN 0-86625-534-6
     1. Indians of North America—Economic conditions—Juvenile literature.
2. Indians of North America—Material culture—Juvenile literature. [1.
Indians of North America] I. Title. II. Series.
E98.E2M33   1994
973'.0497—dc20   94-5528
                                                                          CIP
                                                                          AC

Contents

Introduction

The words "Native Americans" and "Indians" create strong images for many people. Some may think of fierce warriors with bows and arrows, tomahawks, and rifles who battled the U.S. Cavalry in the days of the Wild West. Others probably imagine a proud and peaceful people who just hunted buffalo and lived in tipis on the Great Plains. These are just some of the popular stereotypes of Native Americans, and like most stereotypes they give a false impression.

This series on *Native American Culture* presents six books on various aspects of Native American life: child rearing, arts and crafts, daily life, tribal law, spiritual life, and the invasion by Europe. By reading these books, you will learn that there is no single Native American culture, but instead many different ones. Each Native American group or tribe in the past, as well as today, is a separate nation. While tribes may share some similarities, many are as different from one another as the English are from the Spanish.

The geographic focus of this series is the North American continent (United States and Canada), with special attention to the area within the present-day United States. However, Native Americans have lived, and continue to live, in Central America and South America. In addition, the authors of each book draw upon a wealth of historical information mainly from a time between the 1500s and 1900s, when most Native Americans were first contacted by European explorers, conquerors, and settlers. Much is known about this period of Native American life from documents and observations recorded by Europeans who came to North America.

It is also important to understand that Native Americans have a much longer and more complex history on the continent than just the past 500 years. Archaeologists have excavated ancient Native American sites as old as 12,000 years. The people who lived at these sites were among the first residents of North America. They did not keep written records of their lives, so the only information known about them comes from their stone tools and other remains that they left behind. We do know that during the thousands of years of Native American settlement across the continent the cultures of these early inhabitants changed in many important ways. Some of these cultures disappeared a long time ago, while others have survived and continue to change today. Indeed, there are more than 1.5 million Native Americans currently living in the United States, and the federal government recognizes over 500 tribes. Native Americans are in all walks of life, and many still practice traditions and speak the languages of their ancestors. About 250,000 Native Americans presently live on some 278 reservations in the country.

The books in this series capture the wonderful richness and variety of Native American life from different time periods. They remind us that the story of America begins with Native Americans. They also provide more accurate images of Native Americans, images that I hope will enable you to challenge the stereotypes.

Jordan E. Kerber, Ph.D.
Director of Native American Studies
Colgate University

Daily Differences Among Native American Tribes

*Opposite:
A participant in a California Native American festival shows off the beauty and design of a traditional costume.*

Thousands of years before Columbus and other European explorers reached the Americas, the land was the home of millions of people. When Christopher Columbus went ashore on land now known as the Americas, he thought he had arrived in India. Therefore, he called the native peoples Indians.

Native Americans gathered the wild plants of the Earth for their food. They cultivated crops of corn, squash, pumpkins, beans, and other plants. Deer, buffalo, and many other animals roaming the land provided meat, clothing, tools, and other necessities.

These peoples shared the riches of the land. They took from it only what they needed in order to exist. No one person or group owned land, as we do today. However, they respected the rights of others to control certain territory and occupy it from generation to generation.

*Opposite:
A Seminole family
poses in front of a
group of thatched
structures, constructed
from materials native
to the Florida area.*

Hundreds of tribes of Native Americans lived on the continent when Columbus arrived. We will never know *exactly* what their lives were like before he landed. We have, however, pieced together information about these peoples from the letters and journals of those who first came in contact with them. Also, we have learned about them from the work of archaeologists—scientists who study the cultural and physical remains of early peoples.

How Native Americans lived was determined by *where* they lived. The foods they ate, the animals they hunted, and the kinds of dwellings they constructed all depended upon their natural surroundings—their environment. In this book, we will look at the activities of many different Native American tribes. Each tribe lived in a unique environment. Their habits and customs now serve as excellent examples of how the environment shaped the differences in the tribal ways of Native Americans.

The Eastern Woodlands stretched from what is now New England, across the Great Lakes, into the Ohio River Valley, and south to the Gulf of Mexico. In that region, trees were abundant. The Iroquois and their neighbors made large homes, called longhouses, covered with layers of tree bark. Fishing provided an important source of food for those who lived near the Great Lakes, and deer were plentiful. The Iroquois also planted corn and other crops, and gathered wild plants.

Fishing was not as important to the Sioux, who lived on the Great Plains. That area was like a sea of tall grasses and rolling hills. It stretched from the Mississippi River west to the edge of the Rocky Mountains, and from Canada south to Texas. Trees for building homes were scarce, but thousands of buffalo roamed the land. The people of the Great Plains hunted buffalo and used the hides of these animals to make covers for their homes. In addition to hunting the

Some Native Americans of the Southwest built communities among the rocks and canyons of the area. Here, the ruins of an old village lie beneath the ledges of Canyon De Chelly in Arizona.

buffalo, the southern Sioux (Iowa, Kansa, Omaha, Osage, and other tribes) also foraged (gathered) wild plants.

In the Southwest, the land was mainly desert and had many canyons. Although trees were scarce, there were plenty of stone boulders. The Hopi, and neighboring tribes, in what is now Arizona and New Mexico, used stone and adobe (sun-dried, unburned bricks of clay and straw) to build their homes.

✳

11

The horse also influenced the daily lives of the Native Americans of the West. People of the Great Plains—the Sioux, Cheyenne, Crow, Arapaho, and Comanche, to name a few—were once farmers, hunters, and gatherers. As they learned to appreciate the utility of horses, they gradually stopped farming and began hunting buffalo.

The Native Americans in the Southwest were the first to come in contact with the horse, which is not native to the Americas. Arabian and Andalusian horses were brought to North America by the Spanish, who explored the Southwest and claimed the territory for Spain in the 1500s. When the native people first saw the large animal, they didn't know what to call it. Some called it a big dog, while others named it an elk dog because of its size.

By the late 1600s, the Native Americans of the West had developed new breeds of horses. One tribe became excellent horse breeders. They were the Nez Perce, who lived in the deep valleys of the Bitterroot Mountains in what is now Idaho and Montana. The Nez Perce developed the spotted-rumped Appaloosa. This horse became a prized possession—first of Native Americans, and, later, of the white people.

Trade among the tribes of the West increased after the arrival of the horse. Horses allowed people to travel farther and more easily. People learned more about distant neighbors. They traded a greater amount of goods and learned new skills. In the middle and late 1800s, the horse aided them in their battles against the U.S. Cavalry.

The ways of the early Native Americans showed great creativity, as well as strength and perseverance. They made many contributions to the heritage of the United States and North America. As you read about these peoples and their lives, you may recognize foods, items of clothing, methods of fishing, and even hairstyles that are still with us today.

Chapter

Gathering and Harvesting Plants

Wherever Native Americans lived, they explored the land for edible wild plants, berries, and nuts. Food gathering was often a full-time job in the spring and summer when the land bloomed with new, sweet growth.

Each region of North America offered a distinctive menu, although some areas had more variety than others. In the seasons of plenty, the women gathered just enough for daily use. Depending upon the region, children and some men also gathered foods. As the cold months approached, most Native American tribes preserved food by drying and smoking, and then stored it for leaner times.

In many parts of the country, especially the Southeast and Southwest, the people became skilled farmers. One of their great achievements was discovering how to grow corn, which became a staple of their diet. They also planted squash, beans, pumpkins, and other crops. In the Southwest, they grew cotton. Native Americans ate a variety of plants, some of which we still eat today.

Opposite:
Most Native American peoples of the past traditionally relied on agriculture, hunting, and foraging for their day-to-day survival.

Roots and Wildflowers

In the Southwest, Navajo and Apache women gathered the yucca plant that grew in great abundance. It was called the "desert candle" because it grew very tall, slender, and straight, with a cluster of white flowers at the top.

The stalk of the tender yucca plant was sweet and tasted like asparagus. Young plants could be eaten raw, but older and tougher plants were steamed and stored for the winter.

Steaming was a long process. First, the women dug a large pit and lined it with stones. The fire built in the pit was allowed to burn until only the embers were left and the stones were red hot. The yucca, piled high upon the stones, was covered with wet grass and steamed for a day or more. The steamed plant was then left to dry—wrapped in animal skins and packed in baskets.

After this process was finished, the women prepared additional pits in which to store the dried food for the long winter. The pits were lined with stones and loose brush before the baskets of dried food were placed in them. More loose brush was added to secure the baskets. The openings of the pits were closed with large rocks and sealed with mud. This way, animals could never uncover this treasure!

When spring reached the Pacific Northwest, the women of the Nez Perce, Shoshone, and Chinook tribes set off to gather wild plants, just like their southern neighbors hundreds of miles away. The women of the Pacific Northwest found wild carrots, onions, bitterroot, and sunflower ferns. Their favorite food, however, was the camas bulb.

Camas, a wild lily with beautiful blue blossoms, was a special treat. When the blossoms withered, the plant was dug up with a tool crafted from a willow branch. Uncovering the edible bulb-shaped root took time—but all the work was worth it. The bulb was sweet, juicy, and crunchy. People often ate it raw after first peeling it like an onion.

Camas bulbs were also steamed for long hours in deep pits, much the same way Apache women steamed their harvest of yucca plants. After the bulbs were softened, they were mashed into cakes that could be dried and easily carried as the tribe moved from place to place.

From coast to coast, all Native Americans preserved food by some method of drying. They stored food in a wide variety of containers. Apache women buried their preserved food in baskets. They did not live long in one place, and baskets were easy to transport. Other tribes in the West made clay pots for storage. By contrast, in the Northeast, food was stored in boxes made from birchbark, which was plentiful, long lasting, and waterproof. Northeast tribes also stored food in baskets, pots, and underground pits. In the Southeast, plants grew most of the year. Long-term storage was not as important there.

Piñon Nuts

In autumn, in what is now northern Nevada and Utah, the pine trees released cones with tasty piñon (pronounced pin-yun) nuts. The wandering Paiute people came from far and wide to harvest this special food, which was a staple of their diet. The Paiute and their neighbors, living in the area that is now central California, were considered seed gatherers.

Several scouts usually went ahead to look for groves of trees that had an abundant growth of nuts. When they found a rich spot, the scouts would alert the rest of their party. Once at the grove, the first day of the harvest was devoted to thanksgiving. It was a day of prayer, singing, and dancing to thank the Great Spirit for the rich growth of food that they had been given. Everyone participated in this celebration. The older men led the group, while the young children paraded beside their mothers. The next day the harvest began, and everyone had a job to do.

Before starting to work, each man crafted a tool to reach the pine branches and shake the cones loose. The tool was a long pole made by lashing willow branches together.

The children worked beside their parents. Young boys scrambled up the trees and knocked down cones by hand. As the pine cones covered the ground, the young girls collected the harvest in special baskets, called *kawans*. The older women removed the meat of the nuts from the shells.

Removing the shells took time and skill. The shells were first mixed together with hot stones on a willow tray. Then this mixture was shaken and tossed into the air again and again. Finally, the heat and shaking caused the shells to crack open and the sweet meat to be released. Piñon nuts were often ground and boiled to make a hearty soup.

The annual trip to the mountain slopes for piñon nuts lasted for weeks and sometimes months. It was a time to visit with relatives, as well as harvest food. The old men exchanged stories, while the young men courted their future brides. The women spent time getting to know the children who had been born since the last harvest. It was also a time to discuss tribal matters and choose new leaders.

Wild Rice

Along the western regions of the Great Lakes and into the Mississippi Valley, wild rice grew in great abundance. It was the basic food for many tribes of the area, including the Ottawa, Potawatomi, Sac, Fox, and Winnebago. No group, however, was more skilled at harvesting wild rice than the Menominee. Their name means "wild rice men."

The tall stalks of the wild rice plant grew in shallow water near the shores of lakes and ponds. At the top of each stalk, the seed developed in thick clusters. Before the grain was fully ripe, men and women in canoes paddled among the plants and tied the tops of several stalks together.

This painting by famous American artist Seth Eastman depicts Native Americans gathering rice along the Mississippi River in the 1840s.

A few weeks later, when the rice was ready to harvest, the people set out again in canoes. This time, they slowly drifted through the water and whacked the tops of the plants with sticks, loosening the grains of rice. Some rice fell into the water, ensuring more would grow next season. Most rice, however, fell on mats that lined the bottoms of the canoes.

Back on shore, the rice had to be dried in the sun or over a fire. Then it was threshed—pounded or whacked to separate the edible grain from the tough outer husk. All this hard work was worth the effort. A dish of boiled rice mixed with maple sugar was a tasty treat.

Maple Sugar

Native Americans of the Eastern Woodlands discovered that the maple tree carried a sweet liquid treasure. It could be tapped in the spring and made into maple sugar. Harvesting the sap of the sugar maples was a family affair. After the hunting season ended, a whole village traveled into the deep maple forest and made camp.

Each family was assigned its own stand of trees. One person cut a wide slit in the trunk of each tree, not too far off the ground. Another person pushed a cedar spout into the slit to drain the sap and a birchbark bucket was placed under the spout to capture the liquid as it ran from the tree.

The next step was to place hot stones into the bucket of sticky sap to make it boil and thicken. It was thick enough when solid strings of syrup hung from the stirring paddle. Then it was left to cool and harden. The workers later broke the hardened sugar into clumps that could be easily stored. Only when a family had gathered a year's supply of sugar did they break camp and return home.

Maple sugar was mixed with berries, corn, and a vast array of other ingredients. Mothers even mixed it with children's medicine to make the medicine taste better.

Corn—the Staple of Life

Native American women grind corn in order to prepare sofka, *one of many traditional corn dishes.*

While Native Americans ate many different types of food, their most important food was corn. The Europeans who first came to this continent had never seen corn. The Spaniards named it maize, while the English called it corn. Both learned how to grow the plant from the native peoples and then transplanted it around the world.

It is not known how the Native Americans learned to cultivate corn. It all happened as much as 7,000 years ago. Yet the origin of corn is still a mystery to scientists. Nowhere have they found a wild plant that might be its ancestor.

The kinds of corn we raise today—sweet corn, field corn, and popcorn—were developed by Native Americans. In fact, they developed 150

varieties of corn that grew in different climates. The Mandan tribe living in what is now North Dakota, where summers are short, developed corn that matured in sixty days. In the Southwest, the Hopi and other people of the Pueblo nation developed corn that flourished in hot, dry lands where rainfall was scarce.

The Hopi tribe was the largest of the Pueblo nation. They were probably the world's best farmers because they learned how to transform a near wasteland into productive fields. Somehow, the Hopi discovered that water accumulated underground. They located large pockets of this water and traced its path. Then they placed their fields over these pathways. Farming was also done by complex irrigation networks from rivers, rain runoff, and artificially made reservoirs.

The name Hopi means "the peaceful ones." Tribes did not name themselves. Their names were usually given to them by neighbors and other outsiders. The Hopi probably earned their name because they were too busy to engage in fighting. It is said that the only time the Hopi became hostile was when others stole from their food storehouses.

The Pueblo men did most of the farm work. They planted and harvested corn of all colors—yellow, white, black, blue, pink, and even speckled. The cornstalks grew only three feet high or less, but the yield was plentiful. The Pueblo men also raised beans, squash, and gourds. They even learned to grow the first cotton crops north of Mexico.

In the Eastern Woodlands, planting corn was usually the work of the women because the men were off hunting. The men, however, prepared the fields by digging up the roots and weeds from the last harvest. They also cleared new fields by felling trees or girdling them with deep slashes that caused the trees to rot. In heavily wooded areas, the men could not always clear the fields completely, so the women just planted between trees.

✳

20

Women in the Eastern Woodlands usually planted two corn crops. One was a fast-growing crop that could be eaten during the summer. The other crop ripened in the fall and was dried for winter storage. Beans, squash, pumpkins, and sunflowers were planted in the same rows as the corn. No poles were needed for the beans or sunflowers because the cornstalks, five and six feet tall, made perfect supports.

In the Southeast, the Creek people looked on farming as a family affair. Most of the Creek lived in what is now Alabama, with some in the present-day state of Florida. The weather was hot and humid and people in the area lived on the food they grew. They rarely hunted big game for meat.

Each Creek family had its own farm plot outside of the village. Families also worked cooperatively. In addition to corn and squash, families raised sweet potatoes and melons.

The whole village marched to the farms together. The men carried hoes made with blades of stone or the shoulder bones of animals. The women carried the day's food. The job of the children was to scare away the birds. As the plants grew large, men took turns guarding the fields at night. They didn't want raccoons and other nighttime animals to steal what they had worked so hard to raise.

Wherever corn was grown, people made special regional dishes. In the Southwest, Pueblo and Navajo women ground corn into flour and spread it over a hot stone to make a flat, thin bread, similar to the Mexican tortilla.

In the Southeast, the Cherokee people loved to make corn gruel or porridge and the Creek made corn dough, wrapped it in husks, and boiled it. Sometimes, they fried it in bear grease. In the Northeast, the Iroquois mixed corn with beans and cooked a vegetable stew called succotash.

Along the Great Lakes, the Winnebago tribe prepared corn in many ways. They ate it boiled, roasted, dried, and ground into meal. Their special favorite was steamed corn.

Bags like this were woven from corn husks by the Nez Perce of Idaho. As was common in most Native American cultures, all the elements of a plant or animal were utilized for one purpose or another.

This was prepared in a deep pit that was first lined with hot stones. The pit was filled with corn husks, then a layer of shucked corn, more husks, and finally a light cover of loose dirt. Slowly, water was poured into the pit. As the water hit the hot stones, steam formed and cooked the corn.

The corn plant provided more than food. The husks were perfect for making dolls. Iroquois dolls were faceless. People believed if a doll had a face it might turn into a real person. Husks were also woven into mats or braided into ropes that were used for many purposes.

Even the corncob was put to good use. It could be made into a pipe, a back scratcher, and a scrubber. Dried cobs were burned slowly to smoke fish and meat in order to prevent them from spoiling.

When the late summer or early fall crop was harvested, most tribes in the Northeast and Southeast celebrated the Green Corn Festival. It was a time to give thanks for a good harvest. In Creek country, the ceremony was called the *puskita* or *busk*. The ceremony, which lasted for four days, was also a celebration of the new year.

On the first day of the *busk*, the women cleaned the living quarters, and the men made repairs around the village. All fires were extinguished on the second day, and people fasted to purify themselves. On the next day, they feasted and danced. On the fourth day, the men bathed in the river as part of a special ritual to cleanse themselves of all wrong-doing. Then the shaman, or medicine man, lit the new sacred fires. Four ears of corn were burned and each family restarted its own fire with kindling from the sacred fire.

3

Hunting

Native American men did not hunt for sport. Hunting was a necessity that helped families and whole villages survive. After a big hunt, the women dried and preserved portions of the kill for leaner times. Deer, elk, antelope, bear, moose, and buffalo supplied people not only with food, but with clothing and almost every other necessity.

Deerskin was tanned to make lightweight clothing and saddlebags for journeys on horseback. Bear rugs kept families in the Eastern Woodlands warm at night. A jacket or cloak made of moose hide protected men and women from the frigid winters in the North. Tough buffalo hides made the walls of a Plains tribe tipi resistant to wind, rain, and snow.

Animal bones were converted into tools of every kind— for cutting, sewing, digging, fishing, and scraping animal skins. The insides of animals that were not good for eating were transformed into something useful. A buffalo stomach made a fine cooking pouch for stews and soups.

Opposite:
Buffalo were one of the most important and useful animals for the Plains Indians. These animals were most often hunted on horseback, with bow and arrow.

Hunting Deer

Herds of deer roamed many parts of North America. In the Eastern Woodlands, Mohawk and Seneca men knew the deer trails well. So did the men of the Wampanoag, Pequot, and Delaware tribes. These hunters often laid traps to catch a single deer or smaller animals. A trap was a very efficient way to hunt. Men could be doing other tasks while waiting for the snare to do its work.

One trap was called a deadfall. It was made by hanging a tasty bait from a very heavy log. One end of the log was high off the ground, supported by smaller branches. As soon as the branches were disturbed, the heavy log dropped on the animal and killed it. Another trap was called a snare. It was made by bending a sapling and attaching it to a slip noose. The noose, laid on the ground, enclosed the bait. Once the bait was taken, the trap was sprung.

In many Native American tribes, once a year, during late fall and early winter, the men set out to hunt large numbers of deer. A whole village would move to the hunting grounds and set up temporary dwellings.

Killing deer required more than a good bow, a sharp stone arrow, and a stone-tipped spear. In the less-wooded areas of the East and the mountain fields of the West, deer hunting required patience and silence. Hunters often disguised themselves as deer. They rubbed deer scent over their bodies and wore headpieces of buckskin and antlers. Then each hunter crawled silently into a grazing area.

Sometimes a man got within ten feet of an animal. Crouching low in the grass, a hunter waited for the perfect moment to strike. When the time was right, he stood up quickly and, with his bow steady, sent off a sure shot.

After the kill, the deer had to be skinned. Sometimes skinning took place at the hunting site. Most times, the hunter returned to camp with the deer, where the women helped with the task. Wherever it was performed, the process was similar. First the hide was removed from one side with stone tools called scrapers and the flesh was cut from the bones with stone knives. When the other side was stripped, all the meat was wrapped in the hide until it could be cooked or preserved.

Before the villagers could dine on fresh roasted venison, there was much work to do. Some of the deer meat had to be preserved for the long months ahead. First, it was cut in pieces and laid on racks to dry. The racks were placed high off the ground so that small animals could not snatch the people's hard-won food.

Deer hides provided a durable clothing material for many Native Americans of the Northwest and the Northeast. This beaded buckskin dress was made by a Shoshone in Wyoming.

Next, the meat was smoked to further reduce spoilage. Some pieces were made into jerky—small, dried strips, just the right size to feed hungry travelers. Finally, all of the preserved meat was wrapped tightly in clean skins and packed inside birchbark boxes for safekeeping.

Another job the women handled at camp was scraping and cleaning the hides. With a scraping tool made from other deer bones, the women removed all the fat from one side of the hide. With a stronger tool, they removed the hair from the other side. At a later time, they would tan the hides so the skins could be used for clothing and household items.

Hunting Buffalo

Millions of buffalo once roamed the grass-covered Great Plains, an area that stretches from what is now Canada south to Texas, and from the foothills of the Rocky Mountains across parts of Wyoming, Colorado, the Dakotas, Nebraska, and Kansas. The Native Americans who resided on or near the Great Plains—the Sioux, Cheyenne, Pawnee, Arapaho, Comanche, Kiowa, and Blackfoot, to name a few—survived because of the buffalo. Buffalo provided them with food, clothing, shelter, and just about everything else they needed.

Buffalo hides were transformed into clothing, tipi covers, blankets, drums, and war shields. Woven buffalo hair made strong ropes. Loose hair became stuffing for moccasins, saddle pads, cradle boards used to carry infants, and even large balls used to play games.

The horns of the buffalo were crafted into spoons, bowls, and cups. Small bones became knives. An animal's ribs, tied together with rawhide, made runners for sleds.

A favorite food of the Sioux and their neighbors was a mixture called pemmican. Pemmican comes from the Creek word *pimikan*, meaning "manufactured grease." It was made of strips of sun-dried buffalo meat, fat, and dried berries all pounded together. The dish provided a nutritious, high-protein meal, good for both warriors on the chase and travelers making long journeys. This food could last for several years when stored in special bags and kept dry.

Twice a year, in spring and fall, buffalo ran in large herds of several hundred, and sometimes even thousands. At this time, the people prepared for the great hunt—a hunt that would supply the needs of the families for an entire season.

In the years before Native Americans had horses, hunters chased the buffalo on foot. These hunts were slow and often difficult. The tribes, however, had several methods for capturing large numbers of buffalo without the help of horses. One was the buffalo jump, in which a whole herd was driven over a cliff. Many animals died in the fall. Other buffalo were injured, and so were easy for the hunters to kill.

During a buffalo jump, the buffalo callers had the most dangerous jobs. They were experienced hunters who covered themselves with buffalo hides and mixed with the leaders of the herd. The callers imitated the animals. Just like the buffalo, they snorted and stamped and even rolled over in the grass. The job of the caller was to lure the herd to the edge of the cliff.

Other hunters positioned themselves behind the herd. Upon a special signal, the men in the rear would holler and swirl lighted torches in the air to scare the animals into a stampede. Soon, the rushing herd would be lying at the bottom of the cliff.

Ancient sites on the Great Plains, excavated by archaeologists, contain large stone spear points that were used to hunt extinct buffalo species more than 8,000 years ago. Other sites contain buffalo skeletons that were stampeded into natural traps. One such trap was a dry streambed, called a gulch or arroyo. As the charging buffalo at the front of the stampede tried to cross the gulch, they tripped and were trampled upon by the buffalo running behind them. The hunters quickly followed the fallen herd and easily speared the injured prey. Many stone knives and scrapers have been found at these kill sites indicating that the hunters butchered the animals, cut the meat, and removed the hides.

The surround was another method of hunting large numbers of buffalo on foot. Both men and women took part in this hunt. The women took charge of the dogs, which served as beasts of burden for the Plains people before they had horses. Worker dogs wore harnesses to which long poles were attached to make platforms for dragging goods. A carrying rack was called a travois.

During a surround, the women led the travois dogs to a spot downwind of the herd. There they set up a semicircular fence, which they made by standing the travois poles upright and running cords of animal sinew from pole to pole. Sinew is a strong cord of tissue that attaches a muscle to a bone or other part of the body.

Once the fence was in place, a few brave, fast men positioned themselves on each side of the herd. At the right

Because of their importance in Native American daily life, buffalo were depicted on many objects and pieces of art. Here, two buffalo are the center of a design on a Crow dance shield.

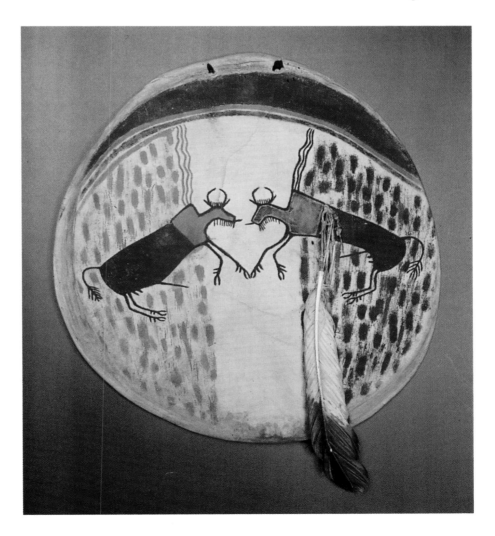

moment, the men started hollering while dodging in and out among the animals. This action caused the buffalo to run in the direction of the fence. Although the fence was too weak to hold the racing animals, something was happening on the other side of the fence that slowed the buffalo in their tracks.

The women and dogs were behind the fence. The dogs barked loudly and jumped in every direction. The women waved shawls in the air. The activity startled the animals at the head of the herd. The large beasts halted or turned and collided with those behind them. Great disorder resulted. Taking advantage of the confusion, men with lances and bows and arrows killed many buffalo.

After the animals were divided among the hunters, the women took down the fences and reassembled the poles on the travois. The travois dogs then dragged the buffalo carcasses back to the village or camp. In the 1700s, horses replaced dogs as carriers of the travois. Then the Plains people could carry more and move farther and faster.

A version of the surround hunting method was also used in other regions to catch large herds of deer and elk. Men built fences three quarters of the way around well-known grazing areas. As large numbers of animals gathered, they became easy captives of the sharp-shooting bowmen.

Making Bows

Not all hunters had bows powerful enough to send arrows long distances. One tribe, the Nez Perce of the Plateau region, became well known for their fine art of bow making. Their best bow was made from the curved horn of the bighorn sheep that roamed the high mountain peaks.

Most bows in the West were made of wood, often ash. The bighorn bow was made from a narrow strip removed from the sheep's horn. The horn material gave the bow long-lasting elasticity. The bow maker first had to reduce the curve in the horn by steaming and stretching it. Then he wrapped it with pieces of sinew. The bighorn bow could shoot an arrow 200 feet—more than twice as far as other bows. While some bows might last a few years, a Nez Perce bighorn bow lasted a lifetime. Men often traded a valuable horse for such a prize.

The bows in the East were usually made from strips of hickory, ash, or oak. The wood was sometimes cut from a log with wedges and scraped with knives made from the teeth of an animal. Sometimes a man might be lucky and find a piece of wood that was the right length and size. Rubbing and shaping were the first steps in bow making. The bow was also greased and left to season. More greasing and drying might be necessary. The bow was not finished until the wood had just the right amount of bend.

Bowstrings were usually made of deer sinew. Several strips of sinew were rolled again and again to make a tight cord. The skin of a snapping turtle's neck made the best bowstring.

Arrowheads were made of stone or any sharp material. Horn, bone, shell, copper, and slate were all used. Stone was an important raw material for making tools . Chipped stone was used for tips of arrows and spears for cutting, butchering, and scraping tools. Common rock types that were used in making chipped-stone tools were flint, quartz, and obsidian (volcanic glass). Ground stone was used to make woodworking tools (axes), sharpening tools (whet-stones), and grinding tools (mortar and pestles). As soon as the Europeans introduced Native Americans to iron, most other materials were abandoned. As a rule, arrowheads were lashed on with sinew. The sinew had to be wet when it was wrapped around the arrowhead and the shaft. When the sinew dried, it shrank and held the arrowhead very tight.

Fishing

Fishing was a less dangerous task than hunting. It required a lot of creativity, however, to find the right technique for different sizes of fish. Native Americans developed a variety of fishing methods that are still used today. They depended on nets of different sizes, wooden traps, hooks, and spears. The spear was frequently combined with other methods.

Along the Great Lakes

Fish were abundant in the Great Lakes and along the rivers of the North that emptied into the Atlantic Ocean. People in those regions fished to supplement hunting, gathering wild plants, and farming.

The Ojibwa (also called Chippewa) and Ottawa who lived at the northern end of Lake Michigan, and the Potawatomi who lived at the southern end near what is now Chicago, perfected the art of fishing with nets. They used

Opposite:
Native Americans who lived near oceans, lakes, and streams found an abundance of food in North America's waters.

nets to capture a large quantity of fish in a short amount of time. Men and women made fishing nets with twine woven from hardy grasses or vines. Nets had different size openings, depending upon the size of the fish to be caught.

A seine is a net to catch small fish. This type of net was held by several people or pulled through the water by a canoe. When the seine net was full with splashing fish, both men and women gathered to spear the fish one by one. As the seine was pulled toward shore, even children got involved. In shallow water, they could catch the small, grounded fish in their hands.

A gill net is a net that is used to catch larger fish. It got its name because the net caught fish by their gill covers and quickly suffocated them. Gill nets are much larger and heavier than seine nets. Native Americans stretched gill nets between poles anchored in a lake or river bottom. One pole was placed close to shore and the other farther out. When the net was full, the far pole was dragged to shore.

Natives of the Great Lakes region also fished by torchlight. They found that light attracted the fish to the surface of the water. It was then easy to spear them at close range.

Fishing with hooks, called gorges, was also common. The hooks were often made from the breastbone of a bird. A gorge was straight, about an inch long with sharp ends. A strong line was tied around the middle of the hook. When a fish swallowed a baited gorge, one end or the other stuck in its mouth.

Some fish, like lake trout and sturgeon, were too large for these nets and hooks. A lake trout might weigh fifty pounds and a sturgeon more than a hundred. For these large fish, fishermen used a weir.

A weir is a fencelike trap that Native Americans built of logs, saplings, and twine. It took time to construct this trap, but it was worth the effort. Wide at one end, the weir

A Hupa stands by a trout trap, also called a weir, waiting to spear a fish as it passes through the narrow opening. Traps, such as this one, were an effective way to harvest the bounty of rivers and streams.

narrowed to a small opening. Only one or two fish at a time could pass through the opening. Standing beside or above the weir, men found it easy to spear the fish.

The Salmon Runs of the Pacific Northwest

The people of the Pacific Northwest, and along what is today the Columbia River, also used weirs to catch salmon. These people were the great fishermen of the continent. They spent most of their time fishing, unlike the Native Americans of the Great Lakes, who also hunted for their food.

Every year, in late spring or early summer, salmon left the Pacific Ocean and swam upstream in the freshwater rivers to lay their eggs and die. The salmon came in great numbers and packed the rivers from bank to bank. The salmon season was a time that people eagerly awaited each year. Whole villages of Tlingit, Haida, Nootka, and Chinook left their winter homes and set up temporary camps near the rivers. They knew there was enough fish to feed their people all year long.

One kind of weir used for salmon was made by adding a funnel-shaped basket to a narrow opening in the fence built across a stream. The basket, made of slender poles, was sometimes twenty feet long. It was wide at one end and closed at the other. The fish never had much chance to escape since their natural instinct was to swim upstream. A fisherman stood on top of the basket and speared the trapped fish one by one.

Native Americans of the Pacific Northwest lived on the large salmon that thrived in the waters. Here, a woman cleans fresh salmon and prepares it for preservation.

✳

A spear used for large fish, like salmon, usually had two or three sharp points rather than one. These tools were made so the pointed ends came off the shaft once a fish was speared. A short line connecting the shaft with the points allowed the heavy fish to thrash around without breaking the shaft. Salmon could weigh as much as fifty pounds.

While the men caught the salmon, the women cleaned the fish. Some would be roasted and eaten day by day. A large portion of the catch had to be preserved for the cold winter ahead. Fish being preserved were first left on drying racks for several days. The catch was usually big, and the racks were piled high with fish. Drying in the sun was not enough to preserve the fish. They were later moved to a hut, where they were smoked.

Giving thanks for this great harvest of riches was an important part of the season. The Chinook held a thanksgiving ritual as soon as the first fish was caught. Like a special guest, a single salmon was set in a place of honor while the men circled around and chanted. Finally, the fish was roasted, and everyone got a small bit to taste.

The ceremony showed reverence and honor for all the fish who were about to sacrifice their lives for their human brothers and sisters. These people, like all Native Americans, believed that everything in nature was connected.

Salmon was not the only kind of fish that was abundant along the Northwest Coast. There were herring, cod, and candlefish. The people used these catches mainly to make fish oil. They boiled the herring and cod and skimmed off the oil and grease.

The candlefish was the main source of oil for the Pacific Northwest tribes. It is said that a dried candlefish was so oily that it could burn like a candle. Maybe that's how it got its name. It was prized and traded far into the interior of the country. These trade routes became known as grease trails.

Homes

The dwelling most commonly associated with Native Americans is the cone-shaped tipi. There were actually many different home styles. Each home style was based on the natural building materials people found in their region.

The tipi was the style used by the people who lived in the Great Plains and in the valleys of the Rocky Mountains. In the Southwest, the people built stone villages on top of rugged cliffs and plateaus, called mesas. Spanish explorers called these villages pueblos, the Spanish word for "town." Hogans, cone-shaped, earth-covered houses, were used by the Navajo. Cedar-plank rectangular houses were also built in the Pacific Northwest, as well as caves and rockshelters that were used by many different groups. One ancient rockshelter—called the Meadowcroft Rockshelter—in what is now western Pennsylvania, has been excavated by archaeologists. They believe that this site was used by a variety of groups of Native Americans for at least 12,000 years. In the Northeast and along the Middle Atlantic coast, many families made their permanent homes in longhouses.

Opposite:
Tipis, such as this one built by the Shoshone, were the most common dwellings for Native Americans of the Great Plains and the Rocky Mountains.

All across the continent, nomadic groups—those who moved frequently—lived in small, dome-shaped shelters. They were easy to construct and could be made quickly with a few bent saplings and loose brush and mats for a cover. Called wigwams or wickiups, they differed from one region to another, but they were generally too small for an adult to stand up in. In the Eastern Woodlands, wigwams were temporary lodgings built for hunting and gathering trips. The wickiup was also used as a sweathouse—a place used for religious steam baths—by the Plains Indians.

Climate also affected the styles of homes that were built by the Native Americans. In the Southeast, families lived in open houses with only a thatched roof to protect them from the sun. During the cool weather, they added walls.

The People of the Longhouse

The Iroquois once lived in the great woodlands along the eastern side of the Great Lakes. The Iroquois nation included the Mohawk, Oneida, Onondaga, Cayuga, and Seneca tribes. The pine, birch, and elm forests offered wonderful building materials for their longhouses.

The name longhouse is a good one because the dwelling was long and narrow. It could be from 50 to 150 feet long and from 18 to 25 feet wide. (Some of the Iroquois longhouses used more than 600 years ago were up to 400 feet long.) The outside the walls were covered with sheets of bark.

Many families lived in one house. Each family was related through the mother. A family had its own space on the two continuous platforms, one above the other, that lined the inside walls. The lower platform was the sleeping space, where a bearskin rug kept family members warm on cold nights. On the upper space, the family kept its few possessions.

Small fires burned day and night most of the year in the open space that ran lengthwise through the center of the house. Two or three families shared one fire for warmth, light, and cooking. The house had no windows, but the domed roof had a hole above each fire through which smoke could escape. When it rained or snowed, the holes could be covered.

Large villages often had fifteen or more longhouses. The village was usually located high on a riverbank and surrounded by a palisade—a high fence made of pointed, slender tree trunks and branches. The palisade protected the villagers from their enemies and provided a high spot for a lookout.

In the Northeast, different tribes adopted the style of the Iroquois longhouse. It was used by many neighboring tribes to the north, such as the Ottawa and Ojibwa. In the Middle Atlantic region, the Delaware and many others in the Algonquian nation favored the longhouse.

The Pueblo Village

A pueblo was the dwelling used by the Hopi, Zuni, and other tribes of the Pueblo nation in the Southwest who settled in present-day Arizona and New Mexico. The nation gets its name from the kind of dwelling it created. The word Pueblo, with a capital letter, is used for the people. Lowercased, the word means the building.

A pueblo was much like a multilevel apartment building made of many one-room units. The men constructed the walls by piling up stone and adobe (sun-dried, unburned brick of clay and straw). Then the women filled the spaces with mud. The inside walls were sometimes plastered with mud made from the clay soil of the area. Although trees were scarce in this part of the country, pueblos usually had wood beams supporting the ceiling.

The clay-like soil of the Southwest has been used for centuries by Native Americans to create everything from pueblo dwellings to jewelry and pottery. Above: Pottery created in the ancient Anasazi style. Right: A ladder that was used to access a kiva, which was a special place built for male members of a pueblo community.

One or two related families lived in a unit. People slept on mats or blankets on the floor. Cooking was done both inside and outside. A pueblo often had no windows or doors. People entered and exited through a hole in the roof. They reached the roof by climbing a ladder that always rested beside the building.

The flat roofs of the pueblos were work spaces. There women made pottery and wove baskets, trays, and hampers to carry food from the fields. Ears of corn were spread out on the flat roofs to dry in the hot sun.

The Pueblo women were probably among the best potters and basket makers in the country. Their homes were filled with storage jars and cooking pots of all shapes and sizes. They put handles on some of the containers and painted designs in many colors on their pots.

Each pueblo village had at least one kiva—a special place only for men. It was a single room built partially underground. There, men gathered to weave cloth for their family's clothing. Sometimes the men used the kiva just to socialize. Most of all, it was a place to hold prayer offerings and religious ceremonies.

A pueblo often stood upon a flat mesa, hundreds of feet above the canyon floor where the villagers raised food and hunted. The villagers carved trails into the steep cliff sides to make their way to and from the bottom of the canyon.

The entrance to an old Anasazi kiva remains intact at the Bandelier National Monument in New Mexico.

Today, some pueblo villages are still used, and others have become history museums. In New Mexico, tourists can visit the ruins of Pueblo Bonito in Chaco Canyon. It was once home to about 1,000 Native Americans known as the Anasazi. In the Navajo language, Anasazi means "alien ancient ones." Pueblo Bonito is about 1,100 years old.

The Tipi of the Plains

The Sioux, Cheyenne, Pawnee, and other Native Americans of the Great Plains traveled long distances, following the buffalo herds. Wherever families journeyed, they carried their tipis. The tipi, also called a lodge, was a woman's responsibility. She made it, set it up, and, when it was time to move, she took it apart and packed it for the trip.

All the women in a village joined together to help a young bride make her new home. The cover of an average-sized tipi was made with ten to fifteen buffalo skins. They were cut and sewn together in the shape of a giant half circle, with additional flaps for the entrance.

When the cover was finished, it was stretched over a cone-shaped frame. At least fifteen poles, each about twenty feet long, were used to form the frame. The main support for the tipi came from three poles set up like a tripod and lashed together at the top. The other poles rested against the tripod, but were firmly anchored in the ground.

In the spring, the women collected straight and slender cedar or fir trees to use as tipi poles. Once the bark was stripped away, each tree was left to dry and season before it could be used as a tipi pole.

The tipi was an ideal lodge for life on the plains. Their buffalo hide covers were strong enough to resist the strong winds that swept across the grasslands. The placement of the dwelling was very important. A tipi's opening always faced east because the powerful winds usually came from the west.

Buffalo-hide tipis, such as these constructed by the Blackfoot, were the most common style of dwelling for Native Americans who inhabited North America's Great Plains.

Inside a tipi, a family lived comfortably. A small fire, covered with stones, kept the day's meal of stew simmering for long hours. A fur-covered buffalo skin made a warm bed that could be rolled up during the day.

Although a tipi might weigh more than 150 pounds, it was a portable home. It could be easily collapsed by pulling out two of the three tripod poles. These poles became a travois for the rest of the tipi, which dragged along the ground. Before the Sioux had horses, the travois was attached to a strong dog. Transporting a tipi became much easier once people owned horses.

The people of the plains often painted murals on the lower walls of a tipi. These wall paintings often told of family events and travels. On the walls of a chief's lodge, skilled painters recreated visions the chief had in dreams or during religious ceremonies. The stories of great battles were also recorded on the walls.

Color pigments for the paints were made from plant and animal materials. To apply these pigments, a painter used various instruments. Willow sticks and chewed cottonwood made excellent penlike tools. Eventually, antelope hair was tied to a twig to make a brush.

Crow and Sioux women also carefully painted designs on buffalo hides used for saddlebags for their horses. These saddlebags, called parfleches, stored food, clothing, and other small items on their journeys.

Clothing

The clothing of the Native Americans, just like their food and homes, depended on how and where they lived. In very hot regions, the people wore as little as possible. In regions that had very cold winters, tribespeople needed fur-covered hides of moose, buffalo, or bear to keep them warm.

Even when clothing was similar, certain things distinguished tribes in one environment from tribes in another. For instance, people on the Great Plains and in the Eastern Woodlands both wore moccasins. The Iroquois, however, stitched their moccasins up the middle, and the Sioux made theirs without a front seam. How these differences came about and why, we may never know, but we can be sure there was a reason behind each method.

Most tribes made at least some of their garments from deerskins. In the Southwest, however, the Hopi people made much of their clothing from the cotton they grew. In other parts of the country, Native Americans did not use cloth until they began trading with the Europeans.

*Opposite:
Geography, natural resources, and climate influenced clothing styles and materials for Native Americans. Here, a group of Hopi women, wrapped in traditional woven blankets, stands on the roof of one of the pueblo dwellings.*

47

As more and more Europeans came to the Americas, the dressing habits of tribes changed. Many Native American tribes slowly adopted some European styles.

Tanning Animal Skins

In both the East and the West, people wore garments made from deerskin. In the West, the skins often came from the elk or antelope, members of the deer family. Before clothes could be crafted from an animal's skin, the hide had to be cleaned and tanned.

The methods used for tanning deer and buffalo hides were similar. Deer hides were tanned mainly for clothing—moccasins, leggings, shirts for men, and dresses or skirts for women. Buffalo hides were tanned and made into tipi covers, circular shields used by warriors, ceremonial headdresses, and carrying bags, such as parfleches.

Women did the tanning work. It was a long process that went on for weeks. First, the flesh side of the animal skin was scraped of all remains. The scraping tool used was made from the shinbone of a deer and shaped to form a sharp edge. Once the skin was clean, it was thoroughly washed and soaked in water for two or three days. The soaking softened the bristles of hair that still had to come off.

The women used a stronger and sharper scraper on the hair-covered side. When tanning buffalo hides for tipi covers, all the fur had to be removed. Usually, hides used for tipi covers came from the summer hunt when the fur was at its thinnest. Fur was not removed from hides with the thickest coats. Those hides were made into large blankets and robes that protected families from the bitter winter cold.

Once both sides of a skin were scraped, they needed to be cured. The women covered the skin with a mixture of fat and liquids from the animal's internal organs, such as the brain and liver, and the hide was soaked in this solution.

After the skin had cured sufficiently, it was stretched on a frame and rubbed with a smooth stone. This part of the process took longer for buffalo hides, which were tougher than deer hides. The buffalo hides had to be soaked, stretched, and rubbed several times before they were soft enough for use.

Deerskin was also smoked for a few minutes, or as much as an hour, to give it some color. The color ranged from cream to dark brown, depending on how long it was smoked. Buffalo skins, on the other hand, were most prized for their whiteness. They were bleached in the sun.

Quills and Beads

Women used their artistic talent to decorate their family's simple clothing. In the Eastern Woodlands, and in many other regions, the most abundant decorative objects found in nature were porcupine quills.

Elaborately quilled buffalo hides, such as this one made by the Dakota, added a colorful and unique decorative dimension to everyday clothing.

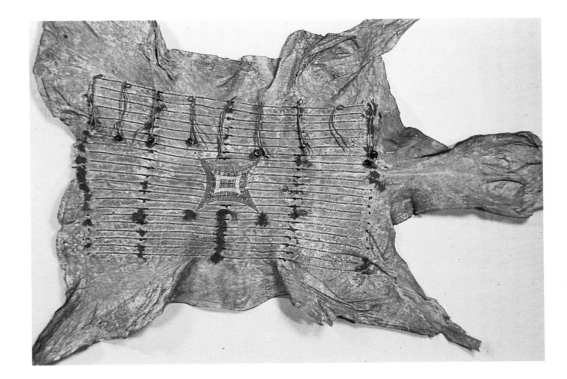

A porcupine quill is hollow, and it can be pulled easily from the animal's back. One animal can provide thousands of quills. They are white with dark tips. Women often colored the quills with berry juice for variety.

Small designs were created by inserting single quills into moccasins, birchbark boxes, and bags made from buffalo skins. Groups of quills could be woven into a braid and attached to leggings and sleeves. Quillwork looked a little like woven straw. It was very strong and long lasting. The quillwork of Ottawa women was highly popular with Europeans. Quillwork pieces more than one hundred years old can be seen in museums today.

Museums also display the beautiful beadwork of the Plains women. They decorated all kinds of garments with porcelain and glass beads. The colorful and shiny beads that transformed their dresses were acquired in trade from Europeans. Before the early 1800s, Plains women, like those in other areas, decorated with quills.

Intricate beadwork, often accompanied by designs painted directly onto an article of clothing, adorned many garments of the Plains Indians. This beaded and painted shirt, made by a Blackfoot woman in Montana, is made in a common Plains style.

The beadwork of the Plains women took many weeks to complete. Beads were either strung together or attached, one by one, onto the deerskin. Instead of thread, the women used sinew. The sinew was made very thin by stretching and rolling it. It was stronger than any modern-day thread.

To attach the beads, the women strung them on sinew and pulled the sinew through holes they had poked in the deerskin. The holes were made with a sharp, pointed tool called an awl, crafted from a tiny bone of an animal. When they began trading with Europeans, the women learned to use steel needles for beadwork.

Deerskin Garments

Men everywhere wore as little as possible in the warm weather. Moccasins and a breechcloth were the basic pieces in a man's wardrobe. A breechcloth, or breechclout, was usually a square of deerskin attached to a hide belt. The deerskin hung like an apron, covering the man both in front and back. Instead of a breechcloth, some men wore a shirtlike garment called a kilt.

Women in the Eastern Woodlands wore deerskin skirts or simple dresses in the summer. Dresses were made of two pieces of deerskin attached at the shoulders and tied around the waist. The women on the plains wore this type of simple dress most of the time. For special occasions, a Plains woman added a top that covered her shoulders and upper arms like a shawl or giant collar. Fringed edges decorated the garments of Plains people, but these borders were less common with other tribes.

Both men and women in the Eastern Woodlands added leggings as the temperature cooled. Their leggings were close fitting and seamed up the front without fringe. They reached from the top of the moccasins to the knee, where they were held in place by a piece of rawhide. Men wore tunic shirts in colder weather. Winter garments for those in the northernmost parts of the Eastern Woodlands included wraps of moose hide, with the fur still in place. Moosehide boots also covered the moccasins.

On the plains, men and women also added deerskin leggings over their moccasins as the weather turned cold. Their leggings were loose fitting, with wide flaps on the outside. This wide style was good for riding horseback.

Deerskin leggings, like these made by the Pawnee of Oklahoma, were worn for extra warmth when the weather on the Great Plains turned harsh and cold.

The chaps that were worn by the early cowboys were probably modeled after the leggings of the plains. When it was bitterly cold, and the Plains families had to leave their warm tipis, they wrapped themselves up in large buffalo blankets that served as fur robes.

In the Southwest, Hopi women wore leggings for their marriage ceremonies and other special occasions. Other times they went barefoot. Leggings and moccasins, unlike those worn by women in other regions, were made from a single piece of hide. It is reported that it took a whole deer hide to make one pair of leggings. Most of the skin was wrapped around their legs several times. When they had finished, their legs looked like the trunks of big trees.

The Hopi men once went barefoot or wore sandals. Then, through trading with neighbors from the plains, they discovered deerskin moccasins. The deerskin offered more protection against the hard, rough pathways between their mesa-top villages and their farms on the canyon floor.

Instead of deerskin, the Hopi villagers wore cotton garments because they were cotton growers and weavers. Men wore short white kilts with woven sashes of many colors. In the cool weather, they added loose shirts made of animal skins—probably elk or antelope. Women wore cotton dresses draped from one shoulder. They, too, wore colorful sashes. The colors and designs on a sash indicated a person's importance in the community.

Hairstyles and Headdresses

Native American men wore their hair in a great variety of styles. Women, on the other hand, had only two main styles—braided or straight. There was, however, one very beautiful exception—the squash blossom worn by a Hopi maiden. This style announced to the village that a girl had reached the marriageable age.

The squash blossom was created by pulling all the hair into two large buns, one on each side of the head. The buns stood for the flowering blossoms of the squash plant. The hairstyle signified that the girl, like the blossom, was about to enter the life-giving, or childbearing, stage. Once the maiden married, she wore her hair in two wide braids. The braids represented the fruit of the mature squash plant.

One common style worn by men was the roach. This style was used by the Mohawk and Seneca of the Eastern Woodlands. Men of less warlike tribes in the same area wore their hair long under small caps topped with two or three feathers.

With a roach, the hair on the sides of the head was singed or plucked away. Only a high strip of hair was left running over the center of the head from front to back. Some men added an artificial roach to make the strip look bigger. Others added one or two feathers. Even in recent times, this style continues to show up now and again on teenage boys.

The traditional Hopi squash blossom hairstyle was worn by young women when they reached childbearing age.

This Navajo boy's shoulder-length hair, held in place by a headband, was typical of a style also worn by the Apache and Hopi.

In the Southeast, Creek men also wore their hair in a roach. Unlike the Mohawk roach, the Creek roach stopped just beyond the crown of the head. The hair in the back was longer and tied like a pony tail. Some men in the Natchez tribe, in what is now Mississippi, were believed to be royalty. They and their attendants wore fancy headdresses over their roaches and collars that resembled those of the pharaohs of ancient Egypt. Cherokee men wore an unusual turban. It was made of colorful cloth obtained from Europeans.

In the Southwest, men often let their hair grow to about shoulder length. It was not braided. A cotton headband worn across the forehead kept it in place. The Hopi men probably started this style, since they were cotton growers. Apache men, neighbors of the Hopi, also preferred a cotton band. Since the Apache did not grow any crops, it is likely that they acquired the cotton cloth by trade or conquest.

On the plains, men usually wore their hair very long and braided. Occasionally they wore an artificial roach, with their own hair pulled into it. The men of the plains also wore the most unusual and beautiful headdresses of all tribes—the eagle feather warbonnet.

The Warbonnet

Only tribes in the West had warbonnets. The Sioux were probably the first to wear them. Sioux bonnets had the longest feather trailers, sometimes reaching to the warrior's feet. The bonnets of the Crow and Nez Perce were much shorter. Only chiefs and other leaders were entitled to wear the bonnet for special ceremonies and war parties.

A warbonnet provided spiritual protection for the wearer in battle. Under the feathers, the man wore a deerskin cap to which feathers were attached. The feathers were tied to one another so they would be held perfectly in place. The trailer with feathers was also attached to the cap.

Each feather in a bonnet carried a story of a great achievement in battle. The achievement was the warrior's ability to touch an enemy in some way. Touching the enemy, and escaping, was more challenging than killing him.

The touch was called a *coup*—a French word that means strike. The feather earned was called a *coup* feather. The warrior or chief would always delight in telling and retelling the saga of how he earned each one.

How did the Sioux and other tribes get enough eagle feathers to decorate all warriors for their bravery? An eagle, after all, is not an easy bird to approach. The method used most often was simple: Steal a young nestling and raise it until he grew the first crop of feathers. When the next set of feathers appeared, they were also plucked. With the third set of feathers, the bird was set free.

Another way to get eagle feathers was more dangerous. It also required a lot of patience. Two young men crawled into pits and covered themselves with grasses. There they waited, with a rabbit for bait, until an eagle flew by. As the eagle swooped down to grasp the rabbit, the men went into action. One grabbed and tied the eagle's feet. The other killed the bird with a fast arrow.

Then and Now

One of the great achievements of the early Native Americans was the ability to live in harmony with nature, using it to meet their needs without destroying it in the process.

Imagine that you live in the village of one of the Native American groups you have just read about. Would you be able to adapt to your environment and find in it all you needed to survive? The daily activities of those early years were physically challenging for Native Americans. Unfortunately, the years that followed were challenging in other ways.

From the 1600s until the 1890s, Native Americans were forced off their lands first by European settlers and then by the U.S. government. Ultimately, many were made to live on reservations. The land on a reservation was often not good for farming or hunting. Native peoples lost their freedom to live in the ways of their ancestors.

Today, some descendants of the early Native Americans live on reservations. Others do not, and are teachers, farmers, doctors, store owners, engineers, politicians, and many other things. It is rare to find Americans who are 100 percent Native American, due to intermarrying. It is common, however, to find many people who have some Native American ancestry. It is a proud heritage to have.

A Sioux stands proudly after having caught an eagle.

Glossary

Appaloosa A type of dappled gray horse with a spotted rump, bred by the Nez Perce tribe of the Northwest.

beadwork The decoration of clothing and other objects using multicolor glass beads. Native Americans in the Great Plains, the Northeast, and the Great Lakes region excelled at creating beadwork.

buffalo jump A method of hunting buffalo in which the animals were driven over a cliff and usually killed.

camas The bulb of the wild lily that was a favorite food of the people of the Northwest.

hogan A house built with logs and sticks and covered with mud or sod; usually cone-shaped. The Navajo people lived in hogans.

kiva Underground ceremonial chambers used by the Pueblo peoples to prepare for ceremonies, store sacred objects, and train shamans.

longhouse The long, narrow, bark-covered dwelling used by the Iroquois and other Eastern Woodlands tribes.

parfleche A type of storage bag that Plains Indians used to carry their belongings.

pemmican A nutritious food made by Sioux and others on the Great Plains from buffalo meat, fat, and berries.

pueblo Native American village made of large clay-brick dwellings. The many Southwest tribes that have lived in these types of houses, such as the Hopi and the Zuni, are known as the Pueblo people.

quillwork The decoration of clothing and other objects with dyed and flattened porcupine quills. Many Native Americans in the Northeast, the Great Plains, and the Great Lakes region were particularly skilled at quillwork.

reservation A tract of land that was set aside by the United States for a group of Native Americans. Usually, reservations were small plots of poor-quality land that were offered to Native Americans only after white settlers had seized their lands.

sweathouse A small building in which religious steam baths are taken; also called a sweatlodge.

tipi A cone-shaped portable house made from a large animal hide cover and a frame of wooden poles. Plains Indians decorated their tipis with paintings.

travois The carrying rack pulled by a dog or horse, used by people of the Great Plains to transport a tipi and other heavy goods.

tribe A group of Native American people who share the same religious, cultural, and social beliefs. When the Europeans first came to North America, there were more than 350 tribes living on the continent.

wickiup A dwelling constructed with poles and covered with brush, grass, or reeds. The Apache lived in wickiups. Plains Indians also used wickiups as sweathouses.

wigwam A dwelling constructed with poles and covered with bark, animal skin, or woven mats. Tribes of the Northeast and Great Lakes used wigwams.

yucca A tall, slender wild plant, called the "desert candle," gathered by Apache and Navajo people.

Further Reading

Bruce, Grant. *Concise Encyclopedia of the American Indian.* Aneval, NJ: Outlet Book, 1989.

D'Apice, Mary. *The Pueblo.* Vero Beach, FL: Rourke, 1990.

Doherty, Craig A., and Katherine M. Doherty. *The Apache and the Navajo.* New York: Franklin Watts, 1991.

_____. *The Crow.* Vero Beach, FL: Rourke, 1994.

_____. *The Huron.* Vero Beach, FL: Rourke, 1994.

_____. *The Ute.* Vero Beach, FL: Rourke, 1994.

Freedman, Russell. *An Indian Winter.* New York: Holiday House, 1992.

Hook, John. *Sitting Bull and the Plains Indians.* New York: Franklin Watts, 1987.

Jenness, Aylette and Rivers, Alice. *In Two Worlds: A Yup'ik Eskimo Family.* Boston, MA: Houghton Mifflin, 1989.

Liptak, Karen. *North American Indian Sign Language.* New York: Franklin Watts, 1990.

Siegel, Beatrice. *Indians of the Northeast Woodlands, Before and After the Pilgrims.* New York: Walker & Co., 1992.

Stan, Susan. *The Navajo.* Vero Beach, FL: Rourke, 1989.

Stein, Conrad R. *The Story of Wounded Knee.* Chicago: Children's Press, 1983.

Wolfson, Evelyn. *From Abenaki to Zuni: A Dictionary of Native American Tribes.* New York: Walker & Co., 1988.

Index

Photo Credits
Cover: ©Renee Lynn/Photo Researchers, Inc.; p. 6: Philippe
Brylak/Liaison USA; pp. 9, 18, 26–27, 35, 36, 45, 46, 54, 55,
57: Library of Congress; p. 10: ©Don Jones/Liaison International; pp. 13, 32: North Wind Picture Archives; pp. 17, 21, 22,
25, 29, 49, 50, 52: ©Blackbirch Press, Inc.; p. 38: ©Renato
Rotolo/Gamma Liaison; p. 42: ©Willa Cather/Photo Researchers, Inc. (left); pp. 42, 43: ©Gene Peach Photography/Liaison
International (right).

Stories of God
AND HIS PEOPLE

A Treasury of Classic Bible Stories

Stories of God
AND HIS PEOPLE

by Arthur W. Gross and A. C. Mueller

Revised and Edited by Rodney L. Rathmann

Illustrated by Glenn Myers

CPH™
SAINT LOUIS

St. Louis

2   3   4   5   6   7   8   9   10   01   00   99   98   97   96   95

The Old Testament

The New Testament

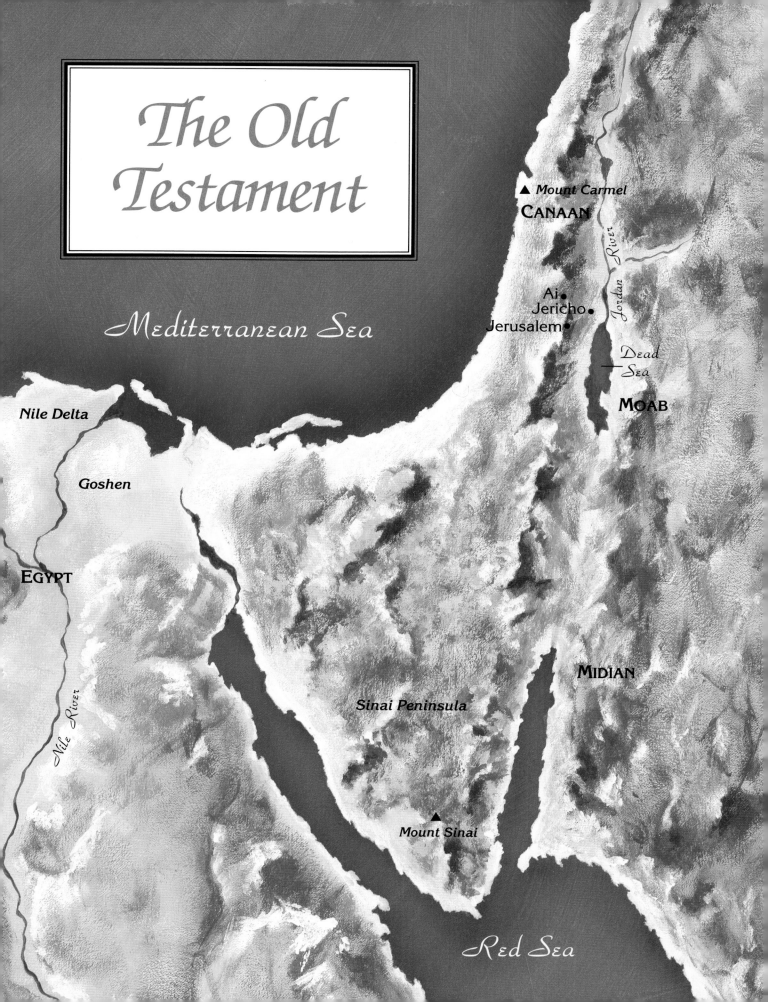

The Old Testament

Mediterranean Sea

▲ *Mount Carmel*

CANAAN

Ai●
Jericho●
Jerusalem●

Jordan River

Dead Sea

MOAB

Nile Delta

Goshen

EGYPT

MIDIAN

Sinai Peninsula

Nile River

▲ *Mount Sinai*

Red Sea

Creation

Genesis 1:1–2:3

This big, wonderful world of ours and all that is in it was made by God. Since at first nothing existed everything had to be created.

But God did not make the world all at once just as we see it now. At first it was a great shapeless mass of land and water mixed together. Everything was wrapped in darkness, and the Spirit of God moved over the waters.

God created everything by the power of His word. Whenever God made something, He simply spoke. And as soon as He had spoken, there it was.

First God made light. Then God divided the light from the darkness and ordered that each should come in turn. God called the light *day*, and the darkness *night*. The light and the darkness together made the very first day.

On the second day God spoke again and made the beautiful blue sky high above us.

On the third day God said, "Let the water under the sky be gathered to one place, and let the dry ground appear."

As soon as God had said this, the waters ran into deep places and formed rivers, lakes, and oceans. Between them dry land appeared.

But nothing grew on the earth. So God commanded the earth to bring forth grass and flowers, vegetables and grain, and bushes and trees of every kind.

The earth was beautiful now, and it was stocked with food for both animals and people.

God saw that it was all very good.

On the fourth day, God spoke again and made the sun, the moon, and the stars. They were to send out light and mark the passing of time—the days, the years, and the seasons.

10

GMYERS

The earth was now ready for living creatures, and on the fifth day God made some of them. He said, "Let the water teem with living creatures, and let birds fly above the earth across the expanse of the sky."

As soon as God had spoken, fish and birds appeared. More creatures were to come. On the sixth day God commanded the earth to bring forth all the kinds of creatures that live on land. He made cattle, wild animals, creeping things, and all the small creatures such as grasshoppers, butterflies, and beetles.

God had created many wonderful things, but His work was not quite finished. The most important and wonderful creatures of all still had to be made.

God wanted human beings on the earth. They were to have it and use it, to enjoy it and take care of it. They were to know and love God, their creator, and live close to Him.

So God made Adam and Eve, a man and a woman. He made them in His own image, holy like Himself. They were the finest and the most beautiful creation of all.

God blessed the man and the woman. "Be fruitful and increase in number," He said. "Fill the earth and subdue it."

God wanted Adam and Eve to have many children, grandchildren, and great-grandchildren. He wanted Adam and Eve to use and care for all He had made.

Now God's work of creation was finished. And so on the seventh day God rested. He blessed this day and made it holy. He looked at His work and rejoiced over it. He declared everything to be very good.

Adam and Eve in Paradise

Genesis 2:8–23

God planted a garden in Eden for Adam and Eve. He made trees that were wonderful to look at and loaded with many kinds of fruit. A river ran through the garden. Flowers sprang up among the grass. Large and small animals played on the ground, the birds flew among the trees and filled the air with song. The Garden of Eden was like a beautiful park. It was Paradise.

Here God put Adam and Eve. Paradise was to be Adam and Eve's earthly home. Here they could live in happiness, taking care of the trees, plants, flowers, and animals.

In the center of Paradise stood a tree called the tree of life, and another tree, called the tree of the knowledge of good and evil. God told Adam and Eve that they might eat of all the trees in the garden except the second tree, the tree of the knowledge of good and evil. "For when you eat of it," He said, "you will surely die."

Adam and Eve were happy in their beautiful garden home. They were good and without sin. God came to them and visited them and talked with them just as a loving father talks with his children. And Adam and Eve loved God.

12

The Fall into Sin

Genesis 3:1–24

Of all the wild creatures God had made, the serpent was the craftiest. One day he came to Eve in the Garden of Eden. He asked her, "Did God really say, 'You must not eat from any tree in the garden?' "

Eve said, "We may eat fruit from the trees in the garden, but God did say, 'You must not eat fruit from the tree that is in the middle of the garden, and you must not touch it, or you will die.' "

"You will not surely die," said the serpent. ". . . you will be like God, knowing good and evil."

Eve looked at the fruit of the tree and saw that it was good. She ate of the fruit and gave some to Adam, and he ate of it also. But at once they found out that the serpent had lied to them. They had disobeyed God. They had sinned. They felt ashamed and tried to hide.

When God asked Adam why he had eaten of the fruit, Adam blamed Eve. When God asked Eve why she had done this, Eve told God that the serpent had lied to her. God cursed the serpent, telling him he would have to crawl on his belly from that time on.

But God promised to send Adam and Eve a Savior. God said that someday the Savior would come and take away the devil's power. God meant that Jesus would come and die on the cross to save all people.

God told Adam that from now on his work would be hard. He told Eve that she would have pain and sorrow. God then told Adam and Eve that, because of their sin, they and all their children would have to die. God drove Adam and Eve out of the garden. He put an angel and a sword of fire at the gate, so they could not come into the garden again.

This is how sin came into the world. Now everything was spoiled. It was no longer good, as it was when God made it.

From Adam to Noah

Genesis 4–5

Adam and Eve found a new home somewhere east of the Garden of Eden. God blessed them with a son named Cain. The Bible tells us that when Cain was born, Eve's heart was filled with joy, for she thought he was the Savior from sin, whom God had promised to send. But soon she was to find out how badly she was mistaken.

Sometime later God sent Adam and Eve another son. They named him Abel.

As the years went by the boys grew up to be young men, and each chose a line of work for himself. Cain became a farmer, Abel a shepherd.

One day both Cain and Abel brought an offering to the Lord. They did this by burning their offerings on an altar made of stone. Cain's offering consisted of products taken from his fields, such as fruit, vegetables, and grain. Abel's offering consisted of some of the best animals of his flock.

God was pleased with Abel's offering, for Abel was sorry for his sin, and he trusted in God to forgive him. But God was not pleased with Cain's offering. This enraged Cain. And one day when Cain and Abel were together in a field, Cain killed Abel.

Then God said to Cain, "Where is your brother Abel?"

Instead of confessing his sin and asking God's forgiveness, Cain boldly lied and said, "I don't know. Am I my brother's keeper?"

God told Cain that the voice of his brother's blood was crying to Him for justice.

Truly, Cain's crime was one that cried to heaven. And the Lord, being just in all His dealings, punished Cain. God told him that the earth, from which he received his food, would no longer produce crops for him. He would have to wander from place to place as long as he lived.

Cain, however, did not repent of his sin. Instead, he gave himself to despair. Cain said, "My punishment is more than I can bear. . . .

whoever finds me will kill me."

God wanted Cain to have time to repent; therefore He mercifully put a mark on Cain. The mark would prevent people from killing Cain.

Cain wandered east into the land of Nod, taking his wife with him. There they had a son whom they called Enoch. In Nod, Cain built a city, which he named Enoch, after his son. In time Cain had many descendants. They were proud and wicked people.

But God gave Adam and Eve another son to take the place of Abel. His name was Seth. Like Abel, Seth was a godly man. He loved the Lord and tried to do what was pleasing to Him. Instead of enjoying sinful pleasures, Seth and his descendants served the Lord and looked forward to the everlasting joys of heaven. Seth was the son from whose descendants the Savior would come.

Adam was 130 years old when Seth was born. Then Adam lived 800 more years, during which time God gave him more sons and daughters. Altogether, Adam lived 930 years, and then he died.

When Seth was 105 years old, he became the father of Enosh. Seth had other sons and daughters and lived 912 years.

Enosh became the father of Kenan and other sons and daughters and lived 905 years.

Kenan was the father of Mahalalel and other sons and daughters and lived 910 years.

Mahalalel became the father of Jared and other sons and daughters and lived 895 years.

Jared became the father of Enoch and other sons and daughters and lived 962 years.

Enoch became the father of Methuselah and other sons and daughters and lived 365 years. And Enoch walked with God. Enoch did not die. God simply took Enoch to live with Him.

Methuselah became the father of Lamech and other sons and daughters and lived 969 years.

Lamech became the father of Noah and other sons and daughters and lived 777 years.

Noah was the father of Shem, Ham, and Japheth.

The Great Flood

Genesis 6:1–9:17

Adam and Eve had children, and their children had children. But all of them were sinful. After a long time there were many wicked people on earth. When God saw this, He was very sad. "I will wipe mankind, whom I have created, from the face of the earth," He said.

But one man, Noah, feared God. He and his wife had three sons. Each of their sons had a wife. So there were eight people in Noah's family.

God told Noah to build an ark, a big ship. He also told Noah to tell the people that God would send a flood to drown them if they did not turn from their sins. God was patient while the ark was being built. But the people did not turn from their sins.

The time for the great flood came. Into the ark Noah put food for the many animals and birds. God sent the animals and birds to Noah, and they went into the ark two by two.

Then Noah and his family went in, and God shut the door. Soon the rain began to fall, and it rained for 40 days and 40 nights. Every living creature, including all the people, drowned. The earth was covered with water. But Noah and his family and the creatures in the ark were saved.

The flood lasted 150 days. Then God sent a wind to dry up the water. When the water went down, the ark landed on a mountain. One day, Noah sent a dove from the window of the ark, and the dove came back with an olive leaf.

A week later Noah sent out the dove again, and it did not come back. Then God told Noah and his family to come out. They had been in the ark a year and 10 days.

Noah built an altar and gave an offering of thanks to God for saving him and his family. God was pleased with the offering and promised Noah that He would never send such a flood again. As a sign of this promise God set the rainbow in the sky.

God saw that the hearts of the people were sinful, even after the great flood. Yet He loved people so much that many years later He sent His only Son, Jesus, to take away their sins.

The Tower of Babel

Genesis 11:1–9

After the flood life on earth began anew.

All Noah's sons and daughters-in-law had children, and when their children grew up and were married, they also had children. And so it continued. The number of people increased rapidly, and soon they had to find more room to live. So the people moved eastward to a broad plain in the land of Shinar and began to build there.

At this time everyone spoke the same language. Everyone understood everyone else.

Although these people, who were the descendants of Noah, knew about the great flood and why God had sent it, they again turned away from Him. They were proud enough to think they could get along without God.

It was God's will that they should spread out and fill the earth. But the people said, "Let us build ourselves a city, with a tower that reaches to the heavens, so that we may make a name for ourselves and not be scattered over the face of the whole earth." Proudly they began work on the city and tower.

God was displeased when He saw what the people were doing. He knew that if the people completed their work, they would become even more sinful. For this reason God stopped the people from continuing

G. MYERS

their building by causing them to speak different languages.

Now the people could not understand one another. They could not work together either. Furthermore, they found it difficult to live together. So they scattered over all the earth, as God had said they should. The city and the tower the people had been building came to be called Babel, for there God had made a "babble," or confusion, of their language.

21

The Call of Abram

Genesis 12; 15; 17

After God confused the language of people at Babel, the human race kept on growing until there were many, many people on earth again. Most of them forgot God and began praying to idols.

In those days there was one man who believed in the true God and would not pray to idols. His name was Abram, and he had a wife named Sarai. Abram was a rich man.

One day God told Abram to go away from his home to a land that He would show him. God promised to give Abram many children, and that from Abram's children's children He would make a great nation. Then God told Abram that He had chosen his family as the people among whom the Savior was to be born.

How hard it must have been for Abram to leave his home and all his relatives and friends! He had to travel far away with his flocks and herds. Abram was 75 years old when he left home.

Abram did not even know the name of the country where he was to go. But Abram loved God and obeyed willingly.

He took his wife and servants and everything he had and went away. He also took his nephew Lot with him. Abram lived in a tent as he moved from place to place.

Finally, Abram came to a land called Canaan, where there was much grass for his sheep and cattle. God told Abram He would give the land of Canaan to Abram's children.

Abram prayed to God often, thanking God for leading him safely to this beautiful land.

God promised Abram that He would keep Abram safe and give him many good things. Yet it seemed strange to Abram that God had not given him any children.

One night God took Abram out under the stars. God told Abram that he would have as many children as there were stars in the sky.

When Abram was 99 years old, God changed his name to *Abraham*, which means "father of many"; He changed Sarai's name to *Sarah*, which means "princess."

Although Abraham did not have even one child, he was sure God would keep His promise and give him many children. Abraham also believed in the promised Savior, and he was happy to know that all his sins were forgiven.

23

God Gives Abraham and Sarah a Son

Genesis 18:1–15; 21:1–8

One day Abraham was resting under a tree outside his tent, for the sun was hot. As he looked up, he saw three men coming, and he ran to meet them. Abraham made a deep bow and invited them to his home.

The men were willing to be his guests; so Abraham ran into his tent and asked Sarah to bake some cakes. Then he sent a servant to prepare a calf for the table. While the men were eating, Abraham stood near them. One of the men was the Lord, the other two were angels.

They asked, "Where is your wife Sarah?"

"There, in the tent," said Abraham.

"I will surely return to you about this time next year," said the Lord, "and Sarah your wife will have a son."

Now Sarah was listening from inside the tent, and when she heard this, she laughed. The thought of having a child, now that she and Abraham were old, seemed funny to her.

"Why did Sarah laugh and say, 'Will I really have a child, now that I am old?' " the Lord asked Abraham. "Is anything too hard for the Lord?"

Sarah became afraid and denied it, saying, "I did not laugh!" But the Lord said, "Yes, you did laugh."

Before another year passed, a son was born to Abraham and Sarah. So God had kept His promise, as Abraham always believed He would.

Abraham and Sarah named their little boy Isaac, which means "laughter," and watched happily as he grew up to be a fine young man.

Abraham and Lot/ Sodom and Gomorrah

Genesis 13:1–18; 14:8–16; 19:1–26

God blessed Abraham in the land of Canaan. He let him become rich in sheep and cattle, gold and silver. Abraham's nephew, Lot, also had flocks and herds and servants.

Both men needed plenty of grass and water for their sheep and cattle. Before long their servants began to quarrel over the land where the grass was best and over the wells of water.

When Abraham heard about this, he said to Lot, "Let's not have any quarreling between you and me, or between your herdsmen and mine, for we are brothers. . . . Let's part company. If you go to the left, I'll go to the right; if you go to the right, I'll go to the left."

God had given Canaan to Abraham. He might have chosen first. But Abraham was a peacemaker; he let Lot choose the land he wanted.

So Lot looked about; and when he saw the rich land near the Jordan River, he chose this good land for himself.

After Abraham and Lot had parted, God came to Abraham again and promised to give the whole land of Canaan to him and his children.

Two cities were near the land Lot had chosen. Their names were Sodom and Gomorrah. The people in these cities were very wicked.

First Lot set up his tent near Sodom; then he moved into the city. Once when four kings came from other lands and carried away Lot and his family, together with the other people of Sodom and Gomorrah, God used Abraham to save them. But the people of Sodom and Gomorrah remained very wicked.

One night two angels came to Sodom. The angels looked like men. When Lot saw them he invited them to his house. They

26

came with Lot and ate with him.

But before everyone went to bed, the men of the city came to Lot's house. They wanted Lot to turn his guests over to them. But Lot stepped outside his house and begged the men not to be so wicked.

When the men of Sodom were planning to break down the door to Lot's house, the angels pulled Lot back inside the house and shut the door. Then they made the men that were at the door of the house blind.

The angels asked Lot, "Do you have anyone else here—sons-in-law, sons or daughters, or anyone else in the city?" Then they told Lot that God was going to destroy the city because of its wickedness.

So Lot went and talked to his sons-in-law, telling them what God was going to do to the city, but they thought he was joking. In the morning when the sun rose, the angels said to Lot, "Hurry! Take your wife and your two daughters. . . . Flee for your lives! Don't look back, and don't stop anywhere in the plain!"

Then the Lord rained on Sodom and Gomorrah burning sulfur from heaven. And the wicked cities were destroyed. Lot's wife did not obey the angels. When she looked back, she became a pillar of salt.

God Saves Abraham's Son

Genesis 22

One day God called to Abraham from heaven. He said, "Take your son, your only son, Isaac, whom you love, and go to the region of Moriah. Sacrifice him there as a burnt offering on one of the mountains I will tell you about."

Abraham obeyed God. Early the next morning he harnessed his donkey, cut wood for the sacrifice, and set out with Isaac and two servants.

On the third day of the journey Abraham could see Moriah in the distance. He stopped and said to his servants, "Stay here with the donkey while I and the boy go over there. We will worship and then we will come back to you."

Now Abraham took the wood and laid it on Isaac, so that he might carry it to the place of the sacrifice. Abraham himself carried the knife and a pot of burning coals.

While the two walked, it struck Isaac that he and his father had everything they needed for the sacrifice except an animal.

"The fire and wood are here, but where is the lamb for the burnt offering?" Isaac asked.

Abraham replied, "God Himself will provide the lamb for the burnt offering." And the two proceeded on their way.

When they came to the place of which God had spoken, Abraham built an altar and arranged the wood on it. Next he tied Isaac and laid him on the wood. Then, in complete obedience to God, Abraham took the knife to kill his son. But at that moment the angel of the Lord called from heaven and stopped him.

"Abraham! Abraham!" He said, "Do not lay a hand on the boy. . . . Now I know that you fear God, because you have not withheld from Me your son, your only son."

Abraham looked up and saw a ram caught in some bushes by its horns, and it could not free itself. Abraham took the ram and offered it as a burnt offering in the place of Isaac.

After this, the angel of the Lord called to Abraham a second time. He reminded Abraham of God's promises to bless him with many descendants, as numerous as the stars in the sky and as the grains of sand on the seashore. Then the angel of the Lord spoke of the Savior, the holy Lamb of God, who would come as one of Abraham's descendants. He would be the perfect—once and for all—sacrifice for the sins of the world. Through Him all nations on earth would be blessed.

29

Isaac's Marriage

Genesis 24

When Abraham's son Isaac grew up, Abraham wanted him to have a good wife. He wanted Isaac to have someone who loved God and would help teach Isaac's children about God. One day Abraham asked his servant to promise that he would go back to Abraham's people and find a wife for Isaac from among Abraham's relatives.

The servant promised he would do what Abraham had asked. He took 10 of Abraham's camels and loaded them with all kinds of presents. Then he started on his long trip.

When he came near the town where Abraham's brother lived, he stopped at the well where the young women of the town came to get water. There he kneeled down and prayed to God. He said, "O Lord, God of my master Abraham, give me success today, and show kindness to my master Abraham." The servant then asked God to let Isaac's future wife be the woman who not only gave him a drink but offered to water his camels too.

While he was still praying, a beautiful young woman named Rebekah came to the well. She was carrying a jar on her shoulder. As soon as she had filled it with water, the servant ran up to her. He said, "Please give me a little water from your jar."

Rebekah gave him a drink right away. Then she said, "I'll draw water for your camels too." So she poured out the rest of her water for the camels and ran back to the well for more.

The servant watched her. She was doing exactly what he had asked God to have the woman do. So he gave her a ring and some other jewelry. Then he asked, "Whose daughter are you?" She told him that she was the granddaughter of Abraham's brother. When the servant heard this, he bowed his head and thanked God for leading him to the right person. Rebekah ran home to tell her family about the man.

As soon as Rebekah's brother heard what had happened, he ran to the well to invite the man to his house. That night, before he would eat, the servant told the whole story of how God had helped him find Rebekah. Rebekah's family allowed her to go with the servant to become Isaac's wife. "This is from the Lord," they said. Soon Abraham's servant and Rebekah were on their way.

As Rebekah came near her new home, Isaac saw the camels coming. Rebekah quickly got down from her camel as Isaac ran to meet her. Then the servant told Isaac all that had happened. So Isaac took Rebekah into his home and married her. And they were very happy.

Isaac Blesses His Children/ Jacob's Ladder

Genesis 25:21–28; 27:1–28:22

God gave Isaac and Rebekah twin sons whom they named Jacob and Esau. Before they were born, God foretold that the older brother would serve the younger. Esau, the firstborn, had coarse and hairy skin. He liked to go hunting, while Jacob was the quiet type who liked to stay around home.

Isaac liked to eat wild game. He loved Esau, but Rebekah loved Jacob.

When Isaac was old and nearly blind, he said to Esau, "Go out into the open country to hunt some wild game for me. Prepare me the kind of tasty food I like and bring it to me to eat, so that I may give you my blessing before I die."

Rebekah heard what Isaac said. When Esau left to go hunting she had Jacob kill two goats, and she made a good meal for Isaac—just the way he liked it. She dressed Jacob in Esau's clothes, covered his smooth skin with goatskin, and told him to take the meal to Isaac. Jacob lied to his father, saying he was Esau.

After Isaac had eaten, he gave Jacob the blessing he had promised to give Esau. When Esau found out that Jacob had received the blessing, he said he was going to kill him.

Rebekah heard about what Esau had said. She called Jacob, telling him to go quickly to her brother's home and stay there until Esau stopped being angry. So Jacob said good-bye to his parents and started out alone.

When night came, he put a stone under his head for a pillow and lay down to sleep. Jacob had a wonderful dream. He dreamed that he saw a ladder standing on the ground and reaching up to heaven.

In Jacob's dream, angels were going up and coming down the ladder, and God was at the top. God said, "I am the Lord, the God of your father Abraham and the God of Isaac. I will give you and your descendants the land on which you are lying. Your descendants will be like the dust of the earth. . . . All peoples on earth will be blessed through you and your offspring." In these words God gave Jacob the promise of the Savior. God told Jacob He would stay with him, watching over him wherever he went.

When Jacob awoke, he said, "This is none other than the house of God; this is the gate of heaven." He set up a stone to mark the place and poured oil on it. He called the place Bethel, which means "house of God."

Jacob promised to serve God all his life and to give back to God one-tenth of all the things God would give him. Then Jacob continued on his journey, happy to know that God had forgiven his wrongs and would always be with him.

33

Jacob and Laban/
Jacob Returns

Genesis 29–33

After Jacob had that wonderful dream, he went on until he came to the land where his mother's relatives lived. There he lived at the home of his uncle, Laban, for 20 years.

Laban had two daughters, Leah and Rachel. Jacob loved Rachel. Laban agreed that Jacob could marry Rachel if Jacob would work for him for seven years. At the end of these seven years, Laban tricked Jacob into marrying Leah instead of Rachel. Then Jacob married Rachel and worked for Laban seven more years for her. So it happened that both of Laban's daughters became the wives of Jacob.

While Jacob worked in Laban's household, God made him very rich. God also gave Jacob 11 sons and a daughter. A 12th son, Benjamin, was born later in Canaan.

At last God told Jacob to go back to the land of Canaan. It was a long and slow journey, for Jacob's servants had to drive all the great flocks and herds belonging to Jacob.

When they came near to the land of Canaan, Jacob remembered how angry Esau had been with him. So he sent messengers to Esau with a friendly greeting.

But the messengers came back to Jacob and told him that Esau was coming with 400 men. Jacob was afraid that Esau would destroy him and his family and take all his goods.

Jacob prayed that God would save him from his brother, Esau. He said, "I am unworthy of all the kindness and faithfulness You have shown Your servant." Jacob knew that all the things he owned had been given him by God.

That night as Jacob was alone at the river, a man came to him and began to wrestle with him. It was God in the form of a man. Jacob knew that he would not win by his own strength, but he would not give up the fight.

He said to the man, "I will not let You go unless You bless me."

Then God blessed Jacob and said, "Your name will no longer be Jacob, but Israel, for you have struggled with God and with men and have overcome."

Then Jacob went to meet Esau and his soldiers. But Esau did not fight with Jacob. Jacob bowed himself to the ground before his brother. Esau ran to meet him, put his arms around him, and kissed him. They both cried for joy.

Then Esau went to his home, and Jacob and his family went to live in the land of Canaan. So it happened that just as God keeps all His promises to us, God blessed Jacob and brought him safely to the Promised Land.

35

Joseph and His Brothers

Genesis 37:1–36

Now Joseph was the second youngest of Jacob's sons, and Jacob loved him more than all his other children. When Joseph's brothers saw the coat of many colors Jacob had made him, they hated Joseph and would not speak a kind word to him.

Then Joseph had two dreams. When he told the dreams to his brothers, they hated him all the more. First he dreamed that he and his brothers were in the field binding sheaves of grain. Joseph's sheaf stood up straight, and all the sheaves of his brothers bowed down to his. Another time he dreamed that the sun, the moon, and 11 stars bowed down to him. These dreams made Joseph's brothers jealous of him.

Later Joseph's brothers were away from home for a long time with their flocks and herds. Jacob said to Joseph, "Go and see if all is well with your brothers and with the flocks." Joseph obeyed his father and went to look for his brothers.

When his brothers saw Joseph coming, they said, "Here comes that dreamer! Come now, let's kill him. . . . Then we'll see what comes of his dreams."

But Reuben, the oldest brother, said, "Don't shed any blood." He suggested instead that they throw Joseph into an empty well. Reuben said this because he wanted to come back later and pull Joseph out of the well and send him back to his father.

When Joseph came up to them, the brothers took his coat of many colors away and put him into the empty well. Then they sat down to eat.

While they were eating, they saw some Ishmaelite merchants who were passing by. One of Joseph's brothers, Judah, said, "What will we gain if we kill our brother and cover up his blood? Come, let's sell him to the Ishmaelites."

So the brothers sold Joseph to the merchants for 20 pieces of silver. The merchants took Joseph far away to Egypt to be sold as a slave.

Joseph's brothers took his coat and dipped it in the blood of a goat and showed it to their father. Jacob knew the coat and thought that a wild animal had killed Joseph. Jacob wept for his dear son.

But God was with Joseph, and many years later both dreams of Joseph came true.

Joseph in Egypt/
Joseph before Pharaoh

Genesis 39:1–41:43

In Egypt, Joseph was sold into slavery. As a slave, Joseph did his work faithfully. Joseph's master saw that God was with Joseph and put him over his whole house.

Now the wife of Joseph's master was a wicked woman. She wanted Joseph to make love to her. But Joseph would not listen. He said, "How then could I do such a wicked thing and sin against God?" Later this evil woman lied to her husband about Joseph. He became very angry and put Joseph into prison.

But God was with Joseph even in prison. Soon the keeper of the prison put Joseph over all the prisoners, because he saw that he could trust Joseph.

Some time after this, two servants of Pharaoh, the king of Egypt, were thrown into prison. The one was Pharaoh's cupbearer, who brought wine to the king. The other was Pharaoh's baker, who baked his bread.

One night both of these men had strange dreams. When Joseph saw that they were sad, he asked them why. They answered, "We both had dreams, . . . but there is no one to interpret them."

Joseph said, "Do not interpretations belong to God? Tell me your dreams."

The cupbearer told his dream, and Joseph gave the meaning: "Within three days Pharaoh will lift up your head and restore you to your position, and you will put Pharaoh's cup in his hand, just as you used to do." Joseph then asked the cupbearer to mention him to Pharaoh when he was back at his job.

The baker also told Joseph his dream, and Joseph gave its meaning: "Within three days Pharaoh will lift off your head and hang you on a tree."

Both dreams came true, just as Joseph had said. But the cupbearer forgot Joseph. And Joseph had to stay in prison two more years.

Then Pharaoh had a strange dream. He dreamed that he saw seven fat cows coming out of the river, followed by seven thin cows, who ate up the fat cows. Later that night the king had another dream. He saw a stalk of grain growing with seven full heads on it. Right after that he saw a stalk with seven empty heads, which ate up the full heads.

When Pharaoh could find no one who could tell him what these dreams meant, the cupbearer, who had been in prison with Joseph, remembered Joseph. He told Pharaoh that Joseph could explain dreams.

Pharaoh sent for Joseph. When Joseph came, Pharaoh asked him whether he could explain dreams. "I cannot do it," said Joseph. "But God will give Pharaoh the answer he desires."

God showed Joseph the meaning of the dreams, so that Joseph could explain them to Pharaoh. He said that both dreams meant the same thing. Egypt would have seven years of great plenty, followed by seven years of famine, when the people would not have enough to eat.

Pharaoh was much pleased with Joseph, so pleased that he made Joseph the second ruler in the kingdom. He put Joseph in charge of gathering food in the seven rich years to be placed in storehouses and saved for the seven poor years.

Pharaoh said Joseph should ride in his second-best carriage. He put his own ring on Joseph's finger and a fine gold chain about his neck. Then Joseph drove through the city and the land, and everywhere the people bowed down before him as the second ruler of Egypt.

Joseph Meets His Brothers/ Israel in Egypt

Genesis 42:1–47:6, 27

Seven years of rich harvests came and went. Then seven years of famine came, just as Joseph had said they would. The famine spread over all of Egypt and over the neighboring lands, including Canaan, where Jacob, 11 of his sons, and their families lived.

When Jacob heard there was grain in Egypt, he sent 10 of his sons to buy some. Jacob did not allow Benjamin, his youngest son, to make the trip, for he feared that some misfortune might come to him as it had to Joseph.

When the brothers arrived in Egypt, they asked where they might purchase grain. They were directed to Joseph.

The brothers bowed low when they met him. Joseph knew his brothers at once. But the brothers had no idea that the high Egyptian official before them, dressed in royal clothes, was Joseph, whom they had sold into slavery about 20 years before. And Joseph did not tell them who he was. He wanted to see whether they were still hateful or whether their hearts had changed.

Then Joseph remembered his dreams. Speaking roughly to his brothers, he accused them of being spies.

Frightened, Joseph's brothers replied, "Your servants were 12 brothers, the sons of one man, who lives in the land of Canaan. The youngest is now with our father, and one is no more."

Joseph pretended not to believe this. He said, "If you are honest men, let one of your brothers stay here in prison while the rest of you go and take grain back for your starving households. But you must bring your youngest brother to me, so that your words may be verified and that you may not die."

Not knowing that Joseph understood them, the brothers began talking among themselves. They reasoned that the trouble they were having was God's punishment for their sin against Joseph.

As Joseph heard all this, the sorrow of the brothers over what they had done brought tears to his eyes. Not wanting the brothers to see his tears, he turned away from them and wept.

But soon Joseph turned back to his brothers and acted like the stern lord again. He had Simeon tied up and put in prison. Joseph also commanded his workmen to fill the sacks of the brothers with grain, put the bag of money each man brought to pay for the grain into the top of his sack, and give the brothers the food they would need on the way home.

On their way home, the brothers' hearts sank when they discovered the money in their sacks. For now, on top of being accused of being spies, they would probably also be accused of being thieves.

When the brothers got home, they told their father all that had happened in Egypt, including the part about Benjamin. But Jacob was still afraid, and again he refused to let Benjamin go to Egypt.

After a while the food Jacob's sons brought home from Egypt was almost gone, and Jacob changed his mind. Sadly he allowed Benjamin to make the trip. To soften the heart of the stern Egyptian official, Jacob had his sons take along gifts and double the money they had taken on the first trip.

The brothers hurried down to Egypt, where again they came face to face with Joseph. At once he sent for his steward. Joseph said, "Take these men to my house, . . . and prepare dinner; they are to eat with me at noon."

Then the steward brought Simeon out of prison and had him join his brothers.

When Joseph came home, the brothers bowed low and gave him the gifts they brought for him. Joseph asked them how they were, and then he said, "How is your aged father you told me about? Is he still living?"

The brothers answered, "Our father is still alive and well."

Then directing attention to Benjamin, Joseph asked, "Is this your youngest brother, the one you told me about?"

Without waiting for an answer, Joseph said to Benjamin, "God be gracious to you."

Joseph was so glad to see Benjamin that tears came to his eyes. To keep his brothers from seeing his tears, Joseph hurried to another room. After he had wept awhile, he washed his eyes and returned to his brothers. Then he gave orders to serve the meal.

Joseph sat at a table by himself, and the brothers were at another table by themselves. Joseph had the steward seat the brothers according to age—first Reuben, the oldest, then Simeon, and so on down to the youngest, who was Benjamin. The brothers noticed this arrangement. How could the Egyptian lord know their ages? they wondered.

Joseph had servants carry portions of food from his table to each of the brothers. But he had them bring five times as many portions to Benjamin as to any of the rest. Joseph did this to show that he wanted to honor Benjamin.

Even though Joseph's brothers had been treated well by Joseph, they were eager to go home.

Knowing this, Joseph said to his steward, "Fill the men's sacks with as much food as they can carry, and put each man's silver in the mouth of his sack. Then put my cup, the silver one, in the mouth of the youngest one's sack."

Early the next morning the brothers started for home. They had gone only a short distance when Joseph sent his steward after them to arrest them. When the steward caught up with the brothers, he accused them in the way Joseph had instructed him.

"Why have you repaid good with evil?" he asked. He said he was looking for his master's silver cup. Imagine how terrified the brothers must have been when the silver cup was discovered in Benjamin's sack!

The only thing the brothers could do was to reload their donkeys and return to Joseph. After the brothers had bowed low before him, he said, "What is this you have done?"

Judah said, "How can we prove our innocence? God has uncovered your servant's guilt. We are now my lord's slaves."

But Joseph said, "Far be it from me to do such a thing! Only the man who was found to have the cup will become my slave. The rest of you, go back to your father in peace."

This was exactly what Judah did not want. If anyone got home, it had to be Benjamin.

So Judah told Joseph all that had happened on the two trips to Egypt, being careful to emphasize their father's grief when Simeon did not return and his fears about Benjamin. Finally Judah said, "Let your servant remain here as my lord's slave in place of the boy, and let the boy return with his brothers. How can I go back to my father if the boy is not with me? No! Do not let me see the misery that would come upon my father."

These words brought tears to Joseph's eyes. Quickly he ordered the Egyptians out of the room, for he did not want them to see him cry. But when the Egyptians were gone, he wept so loud that they heard him. When Joseph could speak again, he said to his brothers, "I am Joseph. Is my father still living?"

What a shock for the brothers! They were so dismayed that they could not say a word. Seeing this, Joseph said, "Come close to me. . . . I am your brother Joseph, the one you sold into Egypt! . . . do not be distressed and do not be angry with yourselves for selling me here, because it was to save lives that God sent me ahead of you."

Joseph told his brothers to hurry and bring their father and all the other members of the family to live in Egypt.

When Pharaoh heard what had happened, he welcomed Joseph's relatives, giving them the best part of Egypt as their home.

When at last the seven years of famine were over, the people planted seed and reaped bountiful harvests again. But Jacob and his family did not return to Canaan. Instead they continued to live in Egypt, where they prospered and increased greatly.

The Birth of Moses

Exodus 1:1–2:10

About 70 people—Jacob, his sons, and their families—moved to Egypt at the time of the great famine. They intended to stay in Egypt only until the famine was over, but instead they and their descendants stayed more than 400 years. During this time they grew into a nation that numbered about two million.

For a long time the rulers and the people of Egypt were kind to the children of Israel, for they remembered Joseph and all he had done to save them from starvation. But years later, long after Joseph was dead and the Pharaoh who knew him was also dead, the Egyptians' kindness came to an end.

The Pharaoh who ruled in these later years became worried because the number of Israelites had grown large and was growing larger. He feared that someday they might join an attacking army and help defeat the Egyptians.

This Pharaoh sought to prevent. He said to his people, "Come, we must deal shrewdly with them or they will become even more numerous."

Pharaoh's way of dealing shrewdly with the Hebrews was to make slaves of them. He set cruel slave masters over them. The slave masters forced the Israelites to build cities and storehouses and work in the fields. Pharaoh hoped that this would weaken the Israelites and reduce their number. But God saw to it that Pharaoh failed in his purpose. The harder the Israelites worked, the more they grew and spread through the land.

Seeing this, Pharaoh tried a different way of weakening the Israelites. He ordered the Hebrew nurses to kill all Israelite boy babies when they were born. But the nurses did not kill the babies. Then Pharaoh ordered his people to throw all Israelite boys into the Nile River as soon as possible after they were born.

About the time Pharaoh gave this order, an Israelite couple from the tribe of Levi had a son. He was a strong, healthy, good-looking little boy. His mother did her best to save him from the Egyptians. For three months she managed to hide him in her home. But when she felt that this would not work any longer, Moses' mother thought of a new plan to hide her baby.

Out of some reeds she made a basket shaped like a boat. She covered it with asphalt and tar to make it waterproof. Then she lined it with soft cloths, put her baby inside, and closed the lid.

Trusting that somehow God would keep her baby safe, she

carried the basket-boat to a place along the river where the princess, Pharaoh's daughter, often came to bathe. There she tenderly set the basket down among the tall reeds that grew near the riverbank and returned home. But Miriam, the baby's sister, stayed nearby to see what would happen to her little brother.

After a while the princess came walking along the river. Soon she noticed the basket in the water. Curious to know what might be inside, she sent one of her maids to get it. Carefully the princess opened the basket. To her great surprise she saw a little Israelite boy—crying. The heart of the princess was touched.

Miriam saw everything that happened. She ran to the princess and said, "Shall I go and get one of the Hebrew women to nurse the baby for you?"

"Yes, go," said the princess.

Miriam ran home and got her mother. The princess said to her, "Take this baby and nurse him for me, and I will pay you."

When the boy was old enough to be away from his mother, she brought him to the palace of the king. There the princess adopted him. She named him Moses.

Thus it was that in the palace of the cruel Pharaoh, who made slaves of the Israelites, there grew up a boy who would someday set them free.

The Call of Moses

Exodus 2:11–4:23

One day, when Moses was about 40 years old, he saw a slave master whipping an Israelite worker. Beside himself with anger, Moses killed the Egyptian and hid him by burying him in the sand.

When news of the murder reached Pharaoh, he became angry with Moses and sought to kill him. Because of this, Moses fled to the land of Midian.

Moses stayed in Midian 40 years. He became a shepherd for a man named Jethro. He also married one of Jethro's daughters, Zipporah.

One day Moses took Jethro's sheep to the grasslands in the neighborhood of Mount Sinai. As he wandered along, he came to a bush that was on fire. But strangely enough the bush did not burn up.

Moses stopped to examine the bush.

"Moses! Moses!" a voice said.

"Here I am," Moses replied.

"Do not come any closer," said the voice. "Take off your sandals, for the place where you are standing is holy ground."

God was speaking to Moses through the burning bush.

Then God told Moses who He was: "I am the God of your father, the God of Abraham, the God of Isaac and the God of Jacob. . . . I have indeed seen the misery of My people in Egypt. . . . and I am concerned about their suffering. So I have come down to rescue them from the hand of the Egyptians and to bring them up out of that land into a good and spacious land, a land flowing with milk and honey. So now, go. I am sending you to Pharaoh to bring My people the Israelites out of Egypt."

Moses said to God, "Who am I, that I should go to Pharaoh and bring the Israelites out of Egypt?"

"I will be with you," God said. "And this will be the sign to you that it is I who have sent you: When you have brought the people out of Egypt, you will worship God on this mountain."

But Moses said, "Suppose I go to the Israelites and say to them, 'The God of your fathers has sent me to you,' and they ask me, 'What is His name?' Then what shall I tell them?"

In answer to this question God explained His name. He said to Moses, "I AM WHO I AM. This is what you are to say to the Israelites: 'I AM has sent me to you.' "

God continued speaking. He told Moses to go to Egypt, to gather the leaders of the tribes of Israel together, and to tell them all that He had said at the burning bush.

Furthermore God told Moses to go with the leaders to the king of Egypt and say to him, "The Lord, the God of the Hebrews, has met with us. Let us take a three-day journey into the desert to offer sacrifices to the Lord our God. "

The Lord also told Moses what would happen after Pharaoh had heard this request: "I know that the king of Egypt will not let you go unless a mighty hand compels him. So I will stretch out My hand and strike the Egyptians with all the wonders that I will perform among them. After that, he will let you go."

"What if they do not believe me or listen to me?" asked Moses.

Still patient, the Lord asked Moses, "What is that in your hand?"

"A staff," Moses answered. He meant his shepherd's staff.

"Throw it on the ground," said the Lord.

When Moses did so, the staff became a snake. Fearful that it might hurt him, Moses fled from it. But the Lord said, "Reach out your hand and take it by the tail."

Moses did as he was told. Then the snake became a staff again.

"This," said the Lord, "is so that they may believe."

Next the Lord said, "Put your hand inside your cloak."

Moses obeyed. When he drew his hand out, it was as white as snow because it was sick with leprosy. But when he put his hand under his cloak again, it became as healthy as it was at first.

"If they do not believe these two signs or listen to you, take some water from the Nile and pour it on the dry ground. The water you take from the river will become blood on the ground."

Moses raised still another objection. He told the Lord that he was not able to speak well and that he did not seem to know what to say. He thought this might hinder him in his work. But the Lord said, "Who gave man his mouth? . . . Is it not I, the Lord? Now go, I will help you speak and will teach you what to say."

Even this did not quiet Moses' fears. "O Lord, please send someone else to do it."

Now the Lord became angry. Sternly He told Moses that Aaron, Moses' brother, who was a good speaker, could speak for Moses. The Lord added that He would help both Moses and Aaron speak and that He would teach them what to say.

At last Moses was ready to answer the call of the Lord and do all He had commanded him. He led his flock back to Jethro and asked for permission to return to Egypt. Jethro said, "Go, and I wish you well."

Moses began his trip to Egypt. His wife and children went along part of the way. After a while Moses met Aaron. Moses was overjoyed to see his brother again. He told him everything the Lord had said. So Moses, at the age of 80, and Aaron, at the age of 83, answered the call of God and returned to Egypt.

Moses before Pharaoh

Exodus 5–10

Moses and Aaron went back to Egypt, as God had directed them. They gathered together the leaders of the tribes of Israel, and Aaron told them all that God had said to Moses.

Moses and Aaron also went to Pharaoh. They said to him, "This is what the Lord, the God of Israel, says: 'Let My people go, so that they may hold a festival to Me in the desert.' "

Pharaoh was proud. Boldly he said, "Who is the Lord that I should obey Him? I do not know the Lord and I will not let Israel go."

Then Moses and Aaron said, "The God of the Hebrews has met with us. Now let us take a three-day journey into the desert to offer sacrifices to the Lord our God, or He may strike us with plagues or with the sword."

But Pharaoh would hear nothing of worship. He didn't want the people away from their work.

The same day Pharaoh told his slave masters not to supply the Israelites with straw to make bricks anymore, as they had been doing. Now the Israelites would have to gather the straw themselves.

"But," Pharaoh added, "require them to make the same number of bricks as before; don't reduce the quota. They are lazy; that is why they are crying out, 'Let us go and sacrifice to our God.' Make the work harder for the men so that they keep working and pay no attention to lies."

The Egyptian slave masters told the people what Pharaoh had commanded. But the Israelites were not able to gather straw and still make the required number of bricks. When the slave masters saw this, they beat some of the Israelites, saying, "Why didn't you meet your quota of bricks?"

Now Moses was in distress. "O Lord," he prayed, "why have You brought trouble upon this people? Is this why You sent me? Ever since I went to Pharaoh to speak in Your name, he has brought

52

trouble upon this people, and You have not rescued Your people at all."

Then the Lord said to Moses, "Now you will see what I will do to Pharaoh: Because of My mighty hand he will let them go."

Moses told the people everything the Lord said. But their suffering was so great that they did not listen to him.

Because Pharaoh, the ruler of Egypt, had defied the Lord by refusing to let the people of Israel leave his country, the Lord sent 10 punishing plagues on Pharaoh and his people.

The first plague came the morning after Pharaoh defied God the first time. Moses and Aaron, following God's command, met Pharaoh on the bank of the Nile River.

Aaron took Moses' rod and struck the water of the river. Immediately it turned into blood. All the fish in the river died, and a stench filled the air. Besides the water of the Nile, the water in the canals, lakes, and ponds of Egypt also turned into blood.

The plague of blood lasted a week. But Pharaoh would not let God's people go.

After the first plague came frogs. And after the frogs came gnats and flies. And after the gnats and flies came a plague that caused all the livestock of Egyptians to die . . . and then another plague that caused the Egyptians themselves to break out in terrible sores.

Even after all this, Pharaoh would not let the children of Israel go.

Then the Lord sent three more plagues, all of which were more severe than the first six. Hail ruined crops and killed livestock and people. Clouds of locusts covered Egypt and ate everything the hail had missed. Finally, three days of darkness covered Egypt from one end to the other. It was so dark that people did not dare move. Only the children of Israel had light where they lived.

Still Pharaoh would not let God's people go.

The Passover and the Exodus

Exodus 11–14

Finally, because Pharaoh would not set Israel free, God said that He would kill every firstborn creature in the land of Egypt, even Pharaoh's firstborn son.

He said that each Israelite family was to kill a lamb and put some of the blood on the sides and tops of the doorframes of their houses. He told the people to roast the meat and eat it quickly with unleavened bread and bitter herbs, wearing their traveling clothes.

Moses and the other people of Israel obeyed. And on the night of this special meal, the Passover meal, God struck down all the firstborn creatures in the land of Egypt, even Pharaoh's firstborn son. But He passed over the houses of the people of Israel with the blood of a lamb on their doorways, and all their firstborn creatures were safe.

Then there was great crying in the land of Egypt and during the night Pharaoh sent for Moses and Aaron. "Up! Leave my people!" he said. Pharaoh wanted them to go quickly. So the people of Israel left Egypt, and they marched out into the desert to worship God.

God went with the people of Israel. During the day He was a cloud that led the way. At night He was a pillar of fire that gave the people light. So they traveled both day and night.

When Pharaoh was told that the people had fled, he and his officials changed their minds. So Pharaoh went after them with his army to bring them back. Pharaoh and his army caught up with the Israelites as they camped by the sea. When the people of Israel saw the Egyptians they were afraid and cried out to the Lord.

But Moses said to the people, "Do not be afraid. Stand firm and you will see the deliverance the Lord will bring you today. . . . The Lord will fight for you; you need only to be still." The pillar of the cloud came between the army of the Egyptians and the camp of Israel. Moses stretched out his hand over the sea; and all that night the Lord drove the sea back with a strong east wind and turned it into dry land. The waters were divided and the people of Israel went through the sea on dry ground with a wall of water on their right and on their left.

The Egyptians came after them and followed them into the sea. The Lord brought confusion upon the Egyptians. The wheels of their chariots came off. And the Egyptians said, "Let's get away from the Israelites! The Lord is fighting for them against Egypt."

And the Lord said to Moses, "Stretch out your hand over the sea." And the sea went back to its place, covering the entire army of Pharaoh. The people of Israel were safe at last. God had delivered them.

God Cares for Israel in the Wilderness

Exodus 15:22–17:6

After the children of Israel had crossed the Red Sea, God led them into the Desert of Shur. For three days they traveled in the desert without finding water. Then they came to Marah. The word *Marah* means "bitter." The water at this place was so bitter that the people could not drink it.

56

The people complained to Moses. Moses took this trouble to God in prayer. The Lord then showed Moses a piece of wood. Moses threw it into the water and the water became sweet.

Soon the food the people had brought with them from Egypt ran out. The people accused Moses and Aaron of leading them out of Egypt only to let them die in the wilderness. They said they were sorry they had ever left Egypt.

Yet God was good to them. He told Moses that He would send them both bread and meat. And He kept His promise in a very wonderful way.

In the evening God sent large flocks of quail to the camp of Israel. There were so many that the people could catch them easily.

Early the next morning God sent Israel the bread that He had promised. When the people rose from their sleep, the ground was covered with little round pieces of food. It tasted like cookies made with honey.

The children of Israel called it *manna*. It was bread from heaven. For 40 years, while they were on the way to the Promised Land, the children of Israel ate this manna.

Now the people were satisfied for a while. But as they traveled, they came to a place where there was no water. God told Moses to strike a certain rock with his rod.

Moses did this and a stream of water flowed from the rock, and all the people could drink.

God always saw to it that His people had food and water as they traveled in the wilderness.

God Gives His People the Ten Commandments

Exodus 19:1–20; 21; 31:18

God wanted the children of Israel to be His people. As He promised to always be with them, He told them what they were to do to show that they were His people.

When the children of Israel had traveled about three months, they came to Mount Sinai. Here God told Moses to tell the people to wash their clothes and be ready for the third day. No one but Moses was to go to the top of the mountain.

58

On the morning of the third day there was thunder and lightning. The people heard a loud trumpet blast. Mount Sinai was covered with smoke, and God had come down to it in fire. The whole mountain shook, and the people were afraid. They stayed at a distance and said to Moses, "Speak to us yourself and we will listen. But do not have God speak to us or we will die."

Then Moses went into the cloud on the mountain, where God was, and God gave Moses two tablets of stone with the Ten Commandments written on them by God Himself.

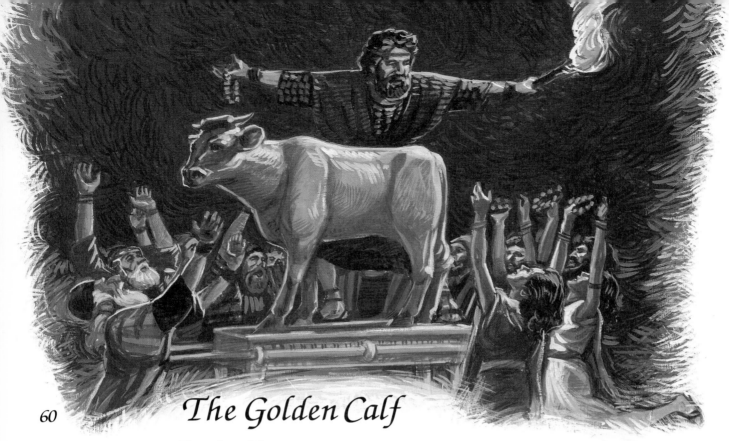

The Golden Calf

Exodus 32

Moses stayed on the mountain 40 days and 40 nights. Down in the camp the people of Israel waited and waited for Moses to return.

Finally an angry mob gathered around Aaron and said, "Make us gods who will go before us. As for this fellow Moses who brought us up out of Egypt, we don't know what has happened to him."

Aaron agreed to do what they wanted. "Take off your gold earrings," he said, ". . . and bring them to me."

The people willingly gave their gold jewelry to Aaron. He melted the gold and shaped it into the form of a calf.

When the idol was finished, the people all said, "These are your gods, O Israel, who brought you up out of Egypt."

When Aaron saw that the people were pleased with the idol, he built an altar in front of it. Then he announced that there would be a great feast on the following day.

The next morning the people got up early. After they had sacrificed burnt offerings on the altar, they ate and drank and then began to sing and dance before the idol.

Then the Lord said to Moses, "Go down, because your people, whom you brought up out of Egypt, have become corrupt. They have been quick to turn away from what I commanded them and have made themselves an idol cast in the shape of a calf. They have bowed down to it and sacrificed to it and have said, 'These are your gods, O Israel, who brought you up out of Egypt.' "

God was very angry with the children of Israel. He also said to Moses, "Now leave Me alone so that My anger may burn against them and that I may destroy them. Then I will make you into a great nation."

At once Moses began to plead for the people. In answer to Moses' prayer God turned away from His anger and decided not to destroy the Israelites.

Now Moses hurried down the mountain. In his hands Moses carried the two stone tablets on which God had engraved His commandments. As soon as Moses came near the camp and saw the calf and the dancing, he became so angry that he threw the stone tablets to the ground, smashing them to pieces. Then Moses destroyed the idol. He threw it into a fire, beat what was left of it to pieces, and ground the pieces to powder. The powder he scattered on the water and made the people drink it.

After this Moses called Aaron and said, "What did these people do to you, that you led them into such great sin?" Aaron tried to excuse himself by blaming the people for the evil that was done.

Thousands of people died because of their sin of idolatry.

Moses pleaded for the people. He asked God to forgive their sin and restore them as His chosen people. God responded, assuring Moses of His faithfulness to His people.

After this God told Moses to cut two stone tablets to replace the ones Moses had broken. When the tablets were ready, Moses carried them up the mountain, and the Lord engraved the same commandments on the new tablets that He had engraved on the first ones.

The People of Israel Worship God

Exodus 25:1–31:11; 35:4–40; 38; Numbers 6:22–26

God had given the Ten Commandments to Israel. But Israel also needed a place of worship. The Lord told Moses that the people should make a holy place for Him because He wished to live among them.

He gave Moses the exact pattern of the holy place. The people lived in tent homes, and God's house was to be a tent too. This tent church was called the tabernacle. It was made to be taken down and set up again.

When Moses came down from the mountain, he called the people together for a meeting. He told them of God's plan, inviting all who were willing to bring an offering for God's house.

The people went home and willingly brought their gold jewelry. They gave silver also, and bronze and wood and linen and skins of animals. Some of the women who knew how to spin made yarn and gave it to Moses. The people offered more than was needed.

Some of the men were skilled in weaving and in working with gold and silver. They had charge of the work and taught others.

These men and their helpers made golden vessels for the tabernacle and hammered some of the gold out in thin sheets.

They made boards and posts and covered them with gold. They wove cloth and made curtains and veils for the tabernacle.

They made a table for the bread of the Presence and an incense altar and a lampstand of gold. They made an altar of bronze and a large basin to hold water for washing.

The finest thing they made was the ark of the Lord. It was a wooden chest covered with gold inside and out. The lid was of gold, and on each end of the lid stood an angel made of gold. Into this ark Moses put the two stone tables with the Ten Commandments written on them.

When the work was finished, Moses set up the boards and spread four curtains over them, to form a tent.

The tent was divided into two rooms by a costly veil. The ark of the Lord was put in the one room, which was called the Most Holy Place. The golden incense altar, the table for the bread of the Presence, and the lampstand were put in the other room, which was called the Holy Place.

Around the tabernacle was a courtyard. Posts were set up around it, and curtains were hung between the posts. A doorway was left open for the priests to enter. In the courtyard stood the altar of burnt offerings and the basin of water.

When everything was ready, Moses burnt incense on the golden altar and offered sacrifices on the altar of burnt offerings. The Lord gave Moses this blessing for Aaron and the other priests to say to the people: *"The Lord bless you and keep you; the Lord make His face shine upon you and be gracious to you. The Lord turn His face toward you and give you peace."*

A cloud also came down and rested on the tabernacle. The cloud showed that the Lord was there. So everyone knew that the Lord had come to live among His people. From that time on the cloud rose out of the tabernacle on the days God wanted the children of Israel to travel. If the cloud did not rise from the tabernacle, the people stayed where they were.

Mutiny and Rebellion

Numbers 13–17

The Lord told Moses to send 12 men—one from each of the tribes of Israel—to explore the land of Canaan.

The men explored the land for 40 days. When they returned, they brought back with them some grapes, pomegranates, and figs.

The men told Moses, "We went into the land to which you sent us, and it does flow with milk and honey! Here is its fruit. But the people who live there are powerful, and the cities are fortified and very large."

Caleb told the people to be quiet. "We should go up and take possession of the land, for we can certainly do it."

But the men who had gone with him said, "We can't attack those people; they are stronger than we are." These men gave bad reports about the land they had explored. "All the people we saw there are of great size. . . . We seemed like grasshoppers in our own eyes, and we looked the same to them," they said.

That night all the people raised their voices. They cried and complained to Moses and Aaron, "If only we had died in Egypt! Or in this desert! We should choose a leader and go back to Egypt."

Moses and Aaron fell face downward before all the people of Israel. Then Joshua and Caleb, two of the men who had explored the Promised Land, the land of Canaan, tore their clothes. They said to the people, "The land we passed through and explored is exceedingly good. If the Lord is pleased with us, He will lead us into that land, a land flowing with milk and honey, and will give it to us. Only do not rebel against the Lord. And do not be afraid of the people of the land, because we will swallow them up. Their protection is gone, but the Lord is with us. Do not be afraid of them."

But the people talked about stoning Joshua and Caleb.

Then the glory of the Lord appeared in the tabernacle before all the people of Israel. And God told Moses about how angry He was that the people of Israel refused to believe in Him. But when Moses asked God to forgive the people, God replied, "I have forgiven them." But as a consequence of their sin, all those from 20 years old and older were not allowed to enter the Promised Land except for Joshua and Caleb. Instead they were forced to wander in the desert for the rest of their lives. Nevertheless, God promised to bring the children of the people into the Promised Land and give it to them for a home.

Some years after that, a man named Korah and his followers came together against Moses and Aaron saying, "You have gone too far! Why do you set yourselves above all the Lord's assembly?" With these words they challenged the authority God had given to Moses and Aaron.

When Moses heard this he said to Korah, "In the morning the Lord will show who belongs to Him and who is holy, and He will have that person come near Him."

The next morning Moses told the people of Israel to move away from the tents of Korah and his followers. Then he said, "This is how you will know that the Lord has sent me. . . . If these men die a natural death . . . the Lord has not sent me. But if the Lord brings about something totally new, and the earth opens its mouth and swallows them, . . . then you will know that these men have treated the Lord with contempt."

When Moses said these words, the ground gave way under Korah and his followers and swallowed them up.

To show that God had chosen Aaron to be a leader of His people, God made buds appear on Aaron's rod. Then Aaron's rod blossomed and produced almonds, just as if it were a live tree.

The Waters of Meribah and the Bronze Snake

Numbers 20:1–21:9

Near the end of Israel's 40 years of wandering in the desert, at a place called Kadesh, the people once again complained because there was no water. Having no faith in God's promise to help them, they gathered around Moses and Aaron and quarreled with them. At once Moses and Aaron hurried to the door of the tabernacle to pray for help. There the glory of the Lord appeared to them. The Lord told Moses to take his rod and gather the people in front of a certain rock. God also told Moses to speak to the rock, for He would overlook the grumbling of the people and give them water.

Moses and Aaron gathered the people before the rock. But then, instead of speaking to the rock, as God had commanded, Moses spoke to the people. In anger and disgust he said to them, "Listen, you rebels. Must we bring you water out of this rock?"

Having said this, Moses did something God had not commanded. With his staff he struck the rock two times. Immediately water gushed out of it. Now the people and their cattle could drink and be refreshed.

Although God supplied water, He was angry with Moses and Aaron, for they had brought water out of the rock in a way different from what He had commanded. Because of this sin, both Moses and Aaron would die before they reached Canaan.

The place where the Lord brought water out of the rock was called *Meribah*. It was given that name because the people had quarreled with God.

The route the Israelites had to take after leaving Kadesh was difficult, and soon the people became impatient and discouraged. So again they complained against Moses and against God. They said to Moses, "Why have you brought us up out of Egypt to die in the desert? There is no bread! There is no water! And we detest this miserable food!"

The Lord punished the people for complaining by sending poisonous snakes among them. The snakes bit the people, causing many of them to die. Then the people realized that they had done wrong and quickly repented of their sin. They went to Moses and said, "We sinned when we spoke against the Lord and against you. Pray that the Lord will take the snakes away from us."

Moses prayed for the people, and the Lord helped them. At the command of God, Moses made a bronze snake. He put this snake on a pole and set it up so that all the people could see it. Then Moses told the people that if those who had been bitten would look at the bronze snake with faith in God's promise to help them, they would get well and live.

Israel Enters the Promised Land

Deuteronomy 30–34; Joshua 1–4

When Moses, the faithful servant of God, had grown old, the Lord told Moses to come to the Tent of Meeting with Joshua. There the Lord appeared in a pillar of cloud. He said to Joshua, "Be strong and courageous, for you will bring the Israelites into the land I promised them on oath, and I Myself will be with you."

With these words God set Joshua apart as the leader of the Israelite people.

The very same day the Lord told Moses to climb Mount Nebo. There he would see the Promised Land, and there he would die.

After blessing the people, Moses climbed Mount Nebo. The Lord showed him Canaan and said, "This is the land I promised on oath to Abraham, Isaac, and Jacob, when I said, 'I will give it to your descendants.' "

When Moses had seen Canaan, he died, and the Lord buried him. Saddened by the death of their leader, the children of Israel wept and mourned for 30 days.

Immediately after Moses' death, Joshua took charge of the people. They accepted him as their leader and did what he commanded.

At this time the children of Israel were encamped a short distance east of the Jordan River. On the far side of the Jordan, a few miles from the Israelite camp, there was a large city named Jericho. It was protected by a high stone wall and strong gates, which were closed every night.

Because Jericho was the first city the Israelites would have to conquer, Joshua sent two spies to explore Jericho and to gather information.

In the evening the spies secretly crossed the river and came to Jericho. There they came to a house owned by a woman named Rahab, where they intended to stay overnight.

But someone saw the spies go to Rahab's house and hurried

to tell the king. Immediately the king sent officers to arrest the spies. The officers said to Rahab, "Bring out the men who came to you and entered your house, because they have come to spy out the whole land."

"Yes," Rahab replied, "the men came to me, but I did not know where they had come from. At dusk, when it was time to close the city gate, the men left. I don't know which way they went. Go after them quickly. You may catch up with them."

The king's officers acted on Rahab's advice. When they had gone away, Rahab hurried to the roof, where she had hidden Joshua's spies. She said to them, "I know that the Lord has given this land to you and that a great fear of you has fallen on us. . . . your God is God in heaven above and on earth below."

Rahab then asked the spies to save her life and the lives of those in her family when the army of Israel entered Jericho. The spies agreed.

To help them escape, Rahab let them down by a rope from an upstairs window that opened to the outside of the city wall.

After hiding in the hills for three days, the spies returned to Joshua and told him everything that happened. Finally they said, "The Lord has surely given the whole land into our hands; all the people are melting in fear because of us." Then Joshua led his people from their camping place to the banks of the Jordan River.

At the end of the three days, Joshua encouraged the people, saying, "Tomorrow the Lord will do amazing things among you."

The next day the priests took up the ark and carried it toward the Jordan. The people came out of their tents and followed it. As soon as the feet of the priests touched the water at the river's edge, the water stopped flowing. It stopped at a point about 10 miles north of the place where the Israelites were. There it piled up and became like a high wall. The water south of this point flowed away into the Dead Sea. So it was that the bed of the river became dry for a distance of about 20 miles.

The priests who carried the ark moved forward until they came to the middle of the riverbed. There they stopped and waited while the Israelites crossed over. When the last of them had crossed, Joshua had 12 men, one from each tribe of Israel, take 12 large stones from the riverbed and carry them to the place where the Israelites were going to spend the night.

After this Joshua said to the priests, "Come up out of the Jordan." As soon as the priests came to the edge of the river and set their feet on its western bank, the water began filling the bed of the river and flowing as before.

At last the Israelites were in Canaan—at home. They pitched their tents and set up the tabernacle at a place called Gilgal, just east of the city of Jericho. There Joshua took the 12 stones his men had taken out of the river and set them up as a memorial. The memorial reminded the Israelites of how they had crossed the Jordan River.

God Gives Israel the Promised Land

Joshua 5:1–24:30

While the Israelites were at Gilgal, Joshua left the camp one day and went near Jericho. As he looked up, he saw a man, sword in hand, standing before him. At first Joshua took him to be just a soldier.

Unafraid, Joshua went up to him and said, "Are you for us or for our enemies?"

"Neither," said the man, "but as commander of the army of the Lord I have now come."

When Joshua realized that his visitor was not just a man, but the commander of God's army of angels, he knelt down and bowed low. Then the commander of God's army assured Joshua that Jericho was as good as captured.

The people of Jericho knew the Israelites were near. So the gates of the city were kept shut. No one was allowed to go out or come in.

God told Joshua precisely what he must do to win Jericho, and

Joshua obeyed. He formed a long procession. First in line were many thousands of armed men. They were followed by seven priests with trumpets made of rams' horns. Then came four other priests, who carried the ark of the Lord. Last in line were more armed men.

Silently, except for the noise of tramping feet and of the continuous blowing of the trumpets, the priests and armed men marched around Jericho once. Then they returned to camp to spend the night. They did this each day for six days.

On the seventh day the Israelites arose at daybreak and began to march again. This time they marched around the city seven times. On the seventh trip the priests sounded a long, loud blast on their trumpets, and Joshua called to the people. "Shout!" he said. "For the Lord has given you the city!"

Instantly all the men shouted. Then, by the power of God, the walls of Jericho fell flat and the city was wide open. The Israelites stormed into Jericho and totally destroyed it, as God had commanded. Nevertheless they spared Rahab and her relatives, as had been promised. They were allowed to live because Rahab had protected the two spies who had come to explore Jericho a few days before.

After Rahab and her family were taken from Jericho, the Israelites burned the city.

The success that Joshua had at Jericho showed that the Lord was with him. And because of the power of the Lord, Joshua's fame spread through all the land.

Joshua led the children of Israel for many years. When he reached the age of 110, he knew he would soon die. Like Moses before him, he also felt that he must speak to the people of Israel once more before death overtook him. He sent messengers through the land and called the people and their leaders to a meeting at Shechem.

Joshua began his address by reminding the people of the victories that God had given them over the tribes in Canaan. He also told them how God would help them in the future by driving away the Canaanites who still remained in the land.

Next Joshua earnestly warned the Israelites against having fellowship with the people of the land and against worshiping their idols. Then Joshua related the history of the Israelite people, always pointing out how graciously and wonderfully God had led them.

"Now fear the Lord and serve Him with all faithfulness," Joshua told the people. "Throw away the gods your forefathers worshiped beyond the River and in Egypt, and serve the Lord. But if serving the Lord seems undesirable to you, then choose for yourselves this day whom you will serve. . . . But as for me and my household, we will serve the Lord."

In reply the people said, "We too will serve the Lord, because He is our God."

Soon afterward Joshua died. The people of Israel buried him close to his home, near the place where they buried the bones of Joseph, which they had taken with them the day they departed from Egypt.

Ruth

The Book of Ruth

Once during a famine in the land of Israel, a man of Bethlehem and his wife, Naomi, moved to the land of Moab with their two sons. There the two sons married Orpah and Ruth, two young women of Moab.

After a time the father died and also the two sons, and Naomi was left alone with Orpah and Ruth. One day Naomi made up her mind to go back to Bethlehem, and Orpah and Ruth got ready and started off with her.

Soon Naomi stopped and said: "Go back, each of you, to your mother's home," for Naomi thought Ruth and Orpah would be happier with their parents. They all wept at the thought of parting. Then Orpah kissed Naomi and went back to the land of Moab.

But Ruth would not let Naomi go on alone: "Don't urge me to leave you or to turn back from you. Where you go I will go, and where you stay I will stay. Your people will be my people and your God my God." So Naomi took Ruth with her, and they came to Bethlehem at the beginning of the barley harvest.

Now Ruth and Naomi were very poor. So Ruth went into a nearby field to gather grain for food. She picked up ears of grain that the reapers let fall.

While Ruth was busy picking up grain, Boaz, the owner of the field, came out. He saw Ruth and asked the reapers who she was. When Boaz learned that Ruth was the young woman who had returned with Naomi from Moab, he invited her to continue working in his field and to drink water from the water jars of his reapers.

After that Ruth came every day to the field of Boaz until all the barley and wheat had been gathered.

Later Boaz married Ruth. God gave them a son, and they called his name Obed. He was the grandfather of King David, of whose family Jesus, our Savior, was born.

The Birth of Samuel

1 Samuel 1:1–2:26

Long ago there lived a man from the hill country of Ephraim who had two wives. His name was Elkanah. The names of his wives were Hannah and Peninnah. Peninnah had children, but Hannah had none. This made Hannah sad, for she wanted very much to have a child.

Once every year Hannah and Elkanah went to the tabernacle in Shiloh. There they prayed and brought an offering to the Lord. Year after year Peninnah would provoke Hannah and irritate her over the fact that she had no children. Whenever Hannah went up to the tabernacle, Peninnah would provoke her till she cried and would not eat.

Elkanah tried to comfort Hannah, but she would not be comforted. Once after they had finished eating and drinking in Shiloh, Hannah stood up. She was very sad and cried as she prayed. She said, "O Lord Almighty, if You will only look upon Your servant's misery and remember me, and not forget Your servant but give her a son, then I will give him to the Lord for all the days of his life."

Eli, the priest, was sitting nearby while Hannah prayed. He saw that her lips moved, but he did not hear her say anything. So Eli thought Hannah was drunk, and he began to scold her.

But Hannah told Eli that she had not been drinking. She explained that she was pouring out her soul to the Lord, praying out of deep anguish and grief.

Eli answered, "Go in peace, and may the God of Israel grant you what you have asked of Him." So Hannah left Eli. She felt better now, and she had something to eat.

Early the next morning Elkanah's family worshiped God and then went back to their home. Sometime afterward God answered Hannah's prayer. He gave her a son, and she was happy. She called him Samuel.

While the baby was very small, Hannah did not go to Shiloh. But she did not forget her promise to God. When Samuel was old enough, she brought him to the tabernacle.

She said to Eli, "I am the woman who stood here beside you

praying to the Lord. I prayed for this child, and the Lord has granted me what I asked of Him. So now I give him to the Lord. For his whole life he will be given over to the Lord."

Hannah thanked God for her son, and after that she and Elkanah went home. But Samuel stayed in God's house. There he began serving the Lord as Eli's helper.

Every year Hannah and Elkanah came to the tabernacle in Shiloh. Each time Hannah brought Samuel a new coat that she had made for him. God blessed Hannah and her husband with three more sons and two daughters, and Samuel grew into a fine young boy.

The Call of Samuel

1 Samuel 2:12–3:21

Now Eli had two sons of his own. They were very wicked. They disobeyed God, and they would not listen to their father when he tried to correct them.

Samuel, however, trusted in God, serving Him in the tabernacle under Eli's instructions.

One night Eli was lying down in his room and Samuel was lying in God's house. Suddenly the Lord called Samuel.

"Here I am," said Samuel. And he ran to Eli and said, "Here I am; you called me."

"I did not call," said Eli. "Go back and lie down."

So Samuel went back and lay down.

Once again the Lord called, "Samuel!"

And Samuel got up and went to Eli and said, "Here I am. You called me."

"My son," Eli said, "I did not call; go back and lie down."

Once more Samuel lay down, and the Lord called Samuel a third time.

So Samuel went to Eli again. This time Eli understood what was happening. He said to Samuel, "Go and lie down, and if He calls you, say, 'Speak, Lord, for Your servant is listening.' "

So Samuel lay down again, and the Lord came and stood there calling as at other times, "Samuel! Samuel!"

Then Samuel said, "Speak, for Your servant is listening."

And the Lord said to Samuel, "See, I am about to do something in Israel that will make the ears of everyone who hears it tingle. At that time I will carry out against Eli everything I spoke against his family—from beginning to end."

The next day Eli made Samuel tell him what God had said.

"He is the Lord," Eli said. "Let Him do what is good in His eyes."

God was with Samuel as he grew up. Samuel learned to know more about God and His love through God's Word.

Saul

1 Samuel 8:1–15:35

Samuel was the judge of Israel for a long time.

When Samuel grew old, his two sons began to assist him with his work. But the sons were dishonest and unfair.

This worried the elders of Israel. They did not want anyone like the sons of Samuel to follow Samuel as judge of Israel. Besides, for some time they had been wanting a king instead of a judge. Now they had an excuse to ask for a king.

The elders of Israel went to Samuel and said, "You are old, and your sons do not walk in your ways; now appoint a king to lead us, such as all the other nations have."

Samuel was displeased. He did not know how to answer the elders. So he prayed for help. The Lord answered him, saying, "Listen to all that the people are saying to you; it is not you they have rejected, but they have rejected Me as their king. . . . Now listen to them; but warn them solemnly and let them know what the king who will reign over them will do."

Following God's directions, Samuel told the elders all that the Lord had said.

The people listened to Samuel, but they paid no attention to his warning. "No!" they said, "We want a king over us. Then we will be like all the other nations, with a king to lead us and go out before us and fight our battles."

Samuel told the Lord all that the elders said. "Listen to them," the Lord replied, "and give them a king."

The man God chose to be king was Saul, the son of a rich man named Kish. Kish and Saul lived in the part of Israel called Benjamin. Saul was a tall, strong, good-looking young man. He was a head taller and more handsome than anyone else in the land.

One day some donkeys that belonged to Kish got lost. He said to Saul, "Take one of the servants with you and go and look for the donkeys."

For two days Saul and the servant searched far and wide, but they found no donkeys. Then Saul said to the servant, "Come, let's go back, or my father will stop thinking about the donkeys and start worrying about us."

But the servant did not like to go home without the lost animals. He said to Saul, "Look, in this town there is a man of God; he is highly respected, and everything he says comes true. Let's go there now. Perhaps he will tell us what way to take."

Saul and the servant climbed the hill to the gate of the town. As they entered the town, they saw Samuel coming toward them. He was on his way to a sacrifice and a feast.

The day before God had spoken to Samuel about Saul: "About this time tomorrow I will send you a man from the land of Benjamin. Anoint him leader over My people Israel."

When Samuel noticed Saul coming toward him, the Lord said to Samuel, "This is the man I spoke to you about."

Samuel said to Saul, "Today you are to eat with me, and in the morning I will let you go and will tell you all that is in your heart. As for the donkeys you lost three days ago, do not worry about them; they have been found."

The next day Samuel took a small bottle of oil and poured some on Saul's head. In this way Saul became king and was put into the service of God.

At first Saul was a good king, but in time he became proud. He was no longer concerned about doing what God commanded. He disobeyed God. He thought he could get along without God.

Saul's disobedience made Samuel angry. He prayed to the Lord about it all night. In the morning Samuel got up early to find Saul. When the two met, Saul said to Samuel, "The Lord bless you! I have carried out the Lord's instructions."

Samuel knew better: "Let me tell you what the Lord said to me last night. Why did you not obey the Lord?"

Saul denied that he had done anything wrong.

But Samuel said, "Because you have rejected the word of the Lord, He has rejected you as king."

Samuel turned to go away. But Saul grabbed his robe to hold him. When he did this, the robe tore. This led Samuel to say, "The Lord has torn the kingdom of Israel from you today and has given it to one of your neighbors—to one better than you."

After that Saul and Samuel never met again.

David Anointed King

1 Samuel 16

Because King Saul had turned away from the Lord, Samuel was brokenhearted. He mourned so long for Saul that the Lord became displeased. He said to Samuel, "How long will you mourn for Saul, since I have rejected him as king over Israel? Fill your horn with oil and be on your way; I am sending you to Jesse of Bethlehem. I have chosen one of his sons to be king."

At first Samuel was afraid to do what God had commanded. He knew that Saul would think of him as a traitor if he would anoint someone to be the king in his place.

Samuel said to the Lord, "How can I go? Saul will hear about it and kill me."

The Lord told Samuel to take a calf with him to Bethlehem and offer it as a sacrifice. He also told Samuel to prepare a feast and to invite Jesse, his sons, and the chief men of their village to the sacrifice and feast. Finally the Lord said, "I will show you what to do."

Then Samuel, no longer afraid, started on his way to Bethlehem.

Jesse had eight sons, but only seven came to the feast. Jesse had them pass before Samuel. When the last of the seven sons had passed before him, Samuel said to Jesse, "Are these all the sons you have?"

"There is still the youngest," Jesse replied, "but he is tending the sheep."

"Send for him," Samuel said.

After a little while the youngest son was brought. His name was David. He was strong and good-looking but still quite young. When he arrived, the Lord said to Samuel, "Anoint him; he is the one."

In keeping with God's command, Samuel took his anointing oil and poured a few drops on David's head. This was the sign that after Saul he would be the king of Israel.

After the feast Samuel returned to his home, and David returned to looking after his father's sheep.

While David was occupied with his sheep, King Saul continued to rule over Israel. But now, since the Lord had rejected him, an evil spirit lived in him. This spirit made him gloomy and filled him with many fears and evil thoughts.

When Saul's officials noticed the change that had come over their king, they went to him and said, "Let our lord command his servants here to search for someone who can play the harp. He will play when the evil spirit from God comes upon you, and you will feel better."

Saul liked this suggestion.

Then one of the king's servants said, "I have seen a son of Jesse of Bethlehem who knows how to play the harp. He is a brave man and a warrior. He speaks well and is a fine-looking man. And the Lord is with him."

Having heard this fine report, Saul sent a message to Jesse, David's father. It said, "Send me your son David, who is with the sheep."

So David entered the service of the king. Whenever the evil spirit troubled Saul, David took his harp and played it for him. The soothing music refreshed Saul and made him calm.

David and Goliath

1 Samuel 17:1–54

The cry of war rang through the land of Israel. The Philistines had come up from their home on the southeastern shore of the Mediterranean and made camp on a hill a few miles northwest of Jerusalem. On another hill, across a valley from the Philistines, King Saul gathered the army of Israel to stop the invasion.

The two armies did not begin to fight at once. Instead a Philistine soldier, a giant named Goliath, came forward every morning and every evening and dared the Israelites to send a man to fight with him, so that the two might decide the outcome of the war.

Goliath was a huge, powerful man, almost 10 feet tall. On his head he wore a helmet of bronze. On his body he wore a coat of mail. To protect his legs, he had strips of metal fastened around them. In his hand he carried a large spear. A javelin was slung across his shoulders. Equipped in this way, Goliath advanced across the valley toward the Israelites. His armor-bearer, carrying his shield, went before him.

When Goliath got close enough to Saul's men to be heard by them, he shouted this challenge: "Why do you come out and line up for battle? . . . Choose a man and have him come down to me. If he is able to fight and kill me, we will become your subjects; but if I overcome him and kill him, you will become our subjects."

Besides challenging the Israelites, the giant also said wicked things against God.

Goliath terrified the soldiers of Israel. They had no one who could match him in size and strength. Every day for 40 days they had to listen to him as he strutted out of the Philistine camp and challenged them.

At this time David was at home tending his father's sheep. But David's three oldest brothers were serving as soldiers in Saul's army. Jesse, their father, began to worry about them. One day he gave David some packages of food and said, "Take this ephah of roasted grain and these 10 loaves of bread for your brothers and hurry to their camp. . . . See how your brothers are doing and bring back some assurance from them."

Early the next morning David took the food and started on his way. When he arrived at the army camp, he left the food with the man who was in charge of supplies. Then he ran to his brothers. While he was talking with them, Goliath came out and challenged the Israelites.

David saw the giant and heard what he said. Standing among the soldiers, David asked, "What will be done for the man who kills this Philistine and removes this disgrace from Israel?"

The men told David what Saul had promised: "The king will give great wealth to the man who kills him. He will also give him his daughter in marriage and will exempt his father's family from taxes in Israel."

84

Then David said to King Saul, "Let no one
lose heart on account of this Philistine; your
servant will go and fight him."

Saul said to David, "You are not able to go out
against this Philistine and fight him; you are only a boy, and
he has been a fighting man from his youth."

But David said, "Your servant has been keeping his father's
sheep. When a lion or bear came and carried off a sheep from the
flock, I went after it, struck it and rescued the sheep from its mouth.
When it turned on me, I seized it by its hair, struck it and killed it. . . .

The Lord who delivered me from the paw of the lion and the paw of the bear will deliver me from the hand of this Philistine."

Then Saul said, "Go, and the Lord be with you."

Saul told his servants to put his armor on David. When this had been done, David tried to move about. But he found he could not.

"I cannot go in these," David said, "because I am not used to them."

David took off the armor. He took his staff and went to the foot of the hill, where he selected five stones at the brook that flowed through the valley. He put the stones into the shepherd's bag that hung at his side. Then, with the sling in his hand and trusting in the Lord for help, David advanced on the giant.

Goliath was insulted when he saw David. He said, "Am I a dog, that you come at me with sticks?"

Goliath cursed David. "Come here," he growled, "and I'll give your flesh to the birds of the air and the beasts of the field!"

But David said to Goliath, "You come against me with sword and spear and javelin, but I come against you in the name of the Lord Almighty."

Now the giant moved in to kill David. And David ran to meet him. David took a stone from his shepherd's bag, laid it into his sling, and hurled it at the giant. The stone sank into his forehead, and Goliath fell unconscious to the ground. David ran up to him, took his sword, and killed him—with Goliath's own sword.

When the Philistines saw that their champion was dead, they fled for their lives. In their hurry they left all their supplies behind. At the same time Saul's men rose up with a shout. They ran after the Philistines, killed many as they fled, and drove them all back into their own country.

When the men returned home after David had killed Goliath, the women from all the towns came out to meet King Saul with singing and dancing. As they danced, they sang:

"Saul has slain his thousands,
and David his tens of thousands."

Saul got very jealous; this song angered him. From then on, Saul kept an eye on David.

David and Saul

1 Samuel 18:6–30, 19:9–18

After Saul, David, and the soldiers of Israel returned home from the battle with Goliath and the Philistines, an evil spirit came forcefully upon Saul. While David was playing his harp for Saul, as he often did, Saul hurled a spear at David. But David escaped.

Saul was afraid of David because he knew the Lord was with him, so he sent David away, giving him command over 1,000 men.

All of Israel loved David because he led them in the war against the Philistines. But Saul hoped David would be killed in battle.

When Saul learned that his daughter Michal loved David, he was pleased. Saul told his servants to tell David that he could marry Michal if he killed 100 Philistines. Saul said this because he hoped the Philistines would kill David. But God was with David, and he and his men went out and killed 200 Philistines so that David could marry Michal. When Saul realized that the Lord was with David and that his daughter Michal loved David, Saul became still more afraid of him, and he remained his enemy for the rest of his life. But David met with more success in battle than any of the rest of Saul's officers, and his name became well known.

Some time after David and Michal were married, an evil spirit once again came upon Saul while David was playing his harp, and Saul tried to pin David to the wall with his spear. But David got away.

Saul then sent men to David's house to watch it and to kill him. But Michal helped David. She let him down through a window, and he escaped. Then Michal took an idol, laid it on the bed, covered it with clothes, and put some goat's hair at the head.

When Saul sent men to capture David, Michal said, "He is ill." Then Saul sent the men back to see David and told them, "Bring him up to me in his bed so that I may kill him." But when the men entered the bedroom, they discovered what Michal had done.

Saul questioned Michal. But David had escaped. He went to stay with Samuel and told him all that Saul had done to him.

David and Jonathan

1 Samuel 18:1–4; 20

David met Jonathan, King Saul's oldest son, when he was brought back to King Saul after killing the giant Goliath. David and Prince Jonathan immediately became close friends.

Moved by his great love for David, Jonathan took off his princely robe and gave it to David. He also gave David his armor, his sword, his bow, and his belt. Then the two young men promised each other that they would always be friends.

Because the Lord was with David, he was successful in everything Saul asked him to do. Saul therefore made David the commander of his army. This pleased the people of Israel.

But Saul soon feared David and watched him carefully. Finally he boldly commanded Jonathan and his servants to put David to death.

Instead of killing David, Jonathan did his best to save David's life.

He went to talk with his father about David. King Saul listened to Jonathan and swore that he would not put David to death.

But Saul soon forgot about his promise. Once again he tried to kill David, and David had to hide from Saul.

One day David met Jonathan secretly. David asked. "What have I done? What is my crime? How have I wronged your father, that he is trying to take my life?"

Jonathan tried to calm David. "Never!" he said. "You are not going to die! Look, my father doesn't do anything, great or small, without confiding in me. Why would he hide this from me? It's not so!"

But David did not feel safe. So Jonathan promised to again find out how King Saul felt about David.

The next day, when Saul and his guests sat down for a feast, David was hiding outside the city. Although David's seat at the table was empty, Saul said nothing. But the day after that, when David still did not appear, Saul asked Jonathan, "Why hasn't the son of Jesse come to the meal, either yesterday or today?"

Jonathan tried to excuse David by telling his father that David had

asked him for permission to go to Bethlehem to be present for a family sacrifice.

Jonathan's answer enraged Saul. He shouted at Jonathan, cursed him, and then tried to kill him with his spear.

The next morning Jonathan went into the field where David was hiding, taking a boy with him. Jonathan said to the boy, "Run and find the arrows I shoot." And he shot several arrows. As the boy ran, Jonathan shot an arrow far over his head. Then he said, "Isn't the arrow beyond you?"

David heard these words and knew that they were a signal that his life was in great danger.

After Jonathan had sent the boy back to the city, David came out of his hiding place. Overcome with love and thankfulness the two kissed each other and wept. Then Jonathan said, "Go in peace, for we have sworn friendship with each other in the name of the Lord."

After this Jonathan returned to the city, and David went away to hide.

David Spares Saul's Life

1 Samuel 22:1–2; 24; 26

David remained in hiding for a long time. And Saul kept trying to find him and kill him. Many who were in distress or in debt or discontented joined David, and he became their leader.

Once Saul went into a cave to relieve himself. David and his men were hiding in the back of the cave. David's men thought God had given David the chance to kill Saul, but David refused. Instead David crept up unnoticed and cut off a corner of Saul's robe. After Saul left the cave, David followed him out and held up the piece of cloth he had cut from Saul's robe. He reminded Saul of his love for him. Saul then praised David for returning his evil actions with acts of kindness and went home. David and his men, however, still stayed away from Saul.

Later King Saul took 3,000 soldiers and hunted for David. One day Saul and his soldiers came very close to David's hiding place. But night came, and King Saul and his men lay down and slept.

David knew that Saul and his men were near. So, with one of his friends, he went to spy on Saul's camp. When they saw that Saul and his soldiers were sleeping, David and his friend walked quietly up to Saul.

David's friend said, "Today God has delivered your enemy into your hands. Now let me pin him to the ground with one thrust of my spear; I won't strike him twice."

But David said, "Don't destroy him! Who can lay a hand on the Lord's anointed and be guiltless?"

Instead of hurting Saul, David took the spear that was sticking in the ground near Saul's head. He also took a jug of water that was lying next to Saul. Then, very quietly, David and his friend crept away.

When Saul realized that once again David could have killed him but didn't, he was ashamed. He promised David that he would stop trying to harm him. "May you be blessed, my son David," said Saul. "You will do great things and surely triumph." Then, taking his soldiers with him, Saul went back to his own home, and David went on his way.

Saul and the Witch of Endor

1 Samuel 28

Some time later Samuel died, and all of Israel mourned for him. After Samuel's death, the Philistine army gathered against the army of Israel. When Saul saw the Philistine army, he was terrified.

Now Saul had expelled from Israel all the people who practiced witchcraft, because witchcraft was against the law of God. Nevertheless Saul decided to break God's law and, disguising himself, went to inquire of a witch at Endor about the outcome of the upcoming battle.

At Saul's request, the witch summoned the spirit of Samuel. As she saw the spirit the woman also recognized the man who stood before her as none other than King Saul.

King Saul addressed the spirit: "I am in great distress," he said, "The Philistines are fighting against me . . . . So I have called on you to tell me what to do."

The spirit replied, "The Lord will hand over both Israel and you to the Philistines, and tomorrow you and your sons will be with me."

Immediately, Saul fell to the ground. He was weak and filled with fear because of Samuel's words and because he had eaten nothing all that day and night.

The witch offered Saul and his men some food, and they ate it. That same night they got up and left.

Saul's Last Day

1 Samuel 31:1–13

As had been predicted, the Philistines defeated the Israelites in battle. Jonathan and his two brothers were killed, and King Saul was wounded by an arrow. Then Saul said to his armor-bearer, "Draw your sword and run me through, or these… fellows will come and run me through and abuse me." When the man refused, Saul fell on his own sword and died. When the armor-bearer saw that Saul was dead, he too fell on his sword and died with him. So King Saul, his three sons, his armor-bearer, and all his men died in battle that day.

David wept when he learned of the death of Saul and Jonathan. David wrote a song about Saul and Jonathan and ordered that it be taught to the men of Judah.

Later David became king. David made Jerusalem his capital city. God was with David, and David ruled the people well.

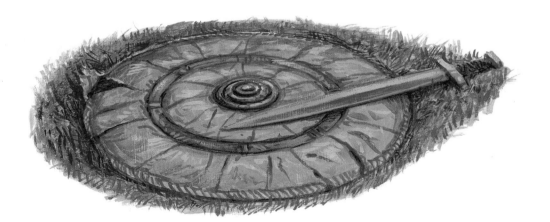

God's Promise to David/David's Prayer

2 Samuel 7

After David settled in his palace, the Lord gave him rest from all his enemies. David said to Nathan the prophet, "Here I am, living in a palace of cedar, while the ark of God remains in a tent."

That night the word of the Lord came to Nathan. God told Nathan to tell David this: "I took you from the pasture and from following the flock to be ruler over My people Israel. I have been with you wherever you have gone, and I have cut off all your enemies from before you. Now I will make your name great, like the names of the greatest men of the earth. And I will provide a place for My people Israel and will plant them so that they can have a home of their own and no longer be disturbed . . . . I will also give you rest from all your enemies . . . I will raise up your offspring to succeed you, . . . and I will establish his kingdom. He is the one who will build a house for My Name, and I will establish the throne of his kingdom forever. . . . Your house and your kingdom will endure forever before Me; your throne will be established forever."

After David heard the words God had spoken to Nathan the prophet, he went in and sat before the Lord. David praised God for fulfilling His promises to him and for the promises He had made that remained for Him to do. David ended his prayer by asking God to continue to bless him and his people forever.

David and Bathsheba

2 Samuel 8; 11–12

When David fought against the enemies of Israel, God gave David every victory. One spring, David sent Joab, the commander of his army, and his men out to battle. But David remained in Jerusalem.

One evening David got up from his bed and walked around on the roof of the palace. From the roof he saw a beautiful woman, Bathsheba, the wife of Uriah, one of David's best warriors, washing herself. Then David sent messengers to get Bathsheba. She came to him and he slept with her.

Later Bathsheba sent a message to David. In the message she told David that she was pregnant.

David sent for Uriah and encouraged him to go home to his wife, so it would look like Bathsheba's child was that of Uriah. But Uriah refused to go home while his fellow soldiers remained on the battlefield.

David then sent word to Joab, saying, "Put Uriah in the front line where the fighting is fiercest. Then withdraw from him so he will be struck down and die."

Later, when Bathsheba heard that Uriah was dead, she mourned for him. When the mourning was past, David brought Bathsheba to his house. Bathsheba became his wife and bore him a son.

What David had done displeased the Lord, and the Lord sent Nathan the prophet to David. Nathan told this story: "There were two men in a certain town, one rich and the other poor. The rich man had a very large number of sheep and cattle, but the poor man had nothing except one little ewe lamb he had bought. . . . Now a traveler came to the rich man, but the rich man refrained from taking one of his own sheep or cattle to prepare a meal for the traveler who had come to him. Instead, he took the ewe lamb that belonged to the poor man and prepared it for the one who had come to him."

David's anger burned against the rich man in Nathan's story. He said, "As surely as the Lord lives, the man who did this deserves to die!"

Nathan said to David, "You are the man! . . . You struck down Uriah the Hittite with the sword and took his wife to be your own." And David said to Nathan, "I have sinned against the Lord."

"The Lord has taken away your sin. You are not going to die," Nathan replied. "But because by doing this you have made the enemies of the Lord show utter contempt, the son born to you will die."

After the firstborn son of David and Bathsheba died, God gave them another son. They named him Solomon, and the Lord loved him.

Absalom

2 Samuel 14:25–18:33

In all of Israel there was no one as handsome as Absalom, the oldest son of King David. From the top of his head to the bottom of his foot he was as handsome as could be.

Absalom said, "If only I were appointed judge in the land! Then everyone who has a complaint or case could come to me and I would see that he gets justice." And whenever anyone approached Absalom to bow down before him, Absalom would reach out his hand, take hold of him, and kiss him. So Absalom stole the hearts of the people of Israel.

After four years, Absalom said to David, "Let me go to Hebron and fulfill a vow I made to the Lord." And David said to him, "Go in peace." So Absalom went to Hebron.

Then Absalom sent spies throughout all the tribes of Israel, saying, "As soon as you hear the sound of the trumpets, then say, 'Absalom is king in Hebron.' " Absalom's plot gained strength, and his following kept on increasing.

Then a messenger came and told David, "The hearts of the men of Israel are with Absalom." And David said to all his officials who were with him in Jerusalem, "Come! We must flee or none of us will escape from Absalom." So David and his household set out immediately.

Absalom and his men came to Jerusalem. Then David and all the people with him crossed the Jordan River. Here David and those with him ate and rested. Then David organized his army. He appointed commanders of thousands and commanders of hundreds. David commanded his captains, saying, "Be gentle with the young man Absalom for my sake."

The battle between Absalom's army and David's army took place in a forest, and Absalom's army was defeated by David's men.

Now Absalom happened to meet some of David's men. He was riding his mule, and as the mule dashed under the thick limbs of a great oak tree, Absalom's head got caught in the branches, and he was left hanging in midair, while the mule he was riding galloped away. Then one of David's commanders, Joab, took three javelins and killed Absalom while he was still hanging in the oak tree. Joab's men took Absalom and threw him into a big pit in the forest and heaped a large pile of rocks over him.

When David learned of the death of Absalom, he was greatly shaken. He wept, saying, "O my son Absalom! My son, my son Absalom! If only I had died instead of you—O Absalom, my son, my son!"

Solomon Receives Wisdom

1 Kings 1–11; 1 Chronicles 28–29; 2 Chronicles 1:1–13

When David was about to die, he made his son Solomon king over all the people of Israel.

One day David called Solomon to him and said, "I am about to go the way of all the earth. So be strong, show yourself a man, and observe what the Lord your God requires: Walk in His ways, and keep His decrees and commands, His laws and requirements, . . . so that you may prosper in all you do and wherever you go." Soon after that David died and was buried in the city of Jerusalem.

Solomon was a young man when he became king. But he remembered what David, his father, had taught him. He remembered how God had loved and helped his father. So Solomon loved God and desired to do His commandments. He also wanted God's help so that he would be a good ruler.

One day Solomon asked his people to go with him to the house of God, which Moses and the people had made long ago as a place of worship. It was in a city called Gibeon. To show his love to God, Solomon gave God a thousand burnt offerings.

That night God spoke to Solomon in a dream. He said, "Ask for whatever you want Me to give you."

Now Solomon could have said: "Give me a long life" or "Give me much money." But he did not ask God for anything like that. Instead, he said, "You have made me king over a people who are as numerous as the dust of the earth. Give me wisdom and knowledge, that I may lead this people, for who is able to govern this great people of Yours?"

God was pleased with Solomon's prayer, because he had asked for wisdom instead of money or something else. God said, "Since you have asked for this, and not for long life or wealth for yourself, . . . I will give you a wise and discerning heart, so that there will never have been anyone like you, nor will there ever be. Moreover, I will give you what you have not asked for—both riches and honor—so that in your lifetime you will have no equal among kings. And if you walk in My ways and obey My statutes and commands as David your father did, I will give you a long life."

When Solomon awoke, he realized that it was a dream. But he believed his dream was true. He went back to his home in Jerusalem and thanked God for His promise. Solomon also gave a feast for all his court.

As with all of His promises, the promise that God made to Solomon came true. Solomon became a great king. He ruled his people well. As long as he lived, his people were safe. From all parts of the world people came to see Solomon and to hear his great wisdom. There was never a man wiser than King Solomon, and God gave him riches greater than any other king of the earth.

Solomon Builds the Temple

1 Kings 5:1–8:66

For more than 400 years the children of Israel had no church except the tabernacle, where the ark of God was kept. David was not allowed to build the temple, but he gathered much gold and silver and many other things that Solomon, his son, could use.

Solomon had been king for four years when he began building the temple. He followed a pattern David had given him from the Lord. The work took seven years. Many workmen cut big cedar trees; others had to cut stones; others worked with gold, silver, and brass.

The temple was built of large stone blocks. As soon as the walls and the roof were up, the inside was covered with cedar boards. Thin sheets of bright gold were spread over the walls, the ceiling, and the floor. The walls and the doors were decorated with figures of angels, palm trees, and flowers.

The temple was divided into two parts. One part was called the Most Holy Place. It contained the ark of God.

Two wooden angels covered with gold faced each other and looked down on the ark. These angels were 15 feet high, and their huge wings spread out wide.

The other part of the temple was called the Holy Place. It had a golden altar for incense, a table made of gold for showbread, the bread of the Presence, and 10 golden candlesticks.

The showbread was 12 loaves of bread laid before the Lord. The bread was changed every Sabbath day.

Between the two parts of the temple hung a beautiful curtain of many colors with figures of angels woven in it.

In front of the temple was a porch. In front of it were two pillars. These Solomon named Jakin and Boaz. Jakin probably means "He establishes" and Boaz probably means "in Him is strength." Outside the temple was an open space called the court. It had a big altar, on which the sacrifices were burned, and a large basin full of water. This large basin was supported by 12 metal bulls.

Solomon invited all the people to Jerusalem for the first service in the temple, and the Lord showed that He was pleased by filling the whole temple with a thick cloud.

Solomon knelt before the altar and asked God to look down in mercy on this house of His, to hear the prayers of the people, and to always be with His people. Solomon also blessed the people, saying, "May the Lord our God be with us as He was with our fathers; may He never leave us nor forsake us. May He turn our hearts to Him, to walk in all His ways and to keep the commands, decrees, and regulations He gave our fathers. And may these words of mine, which I have prayed before the Lord, be near to the Lord our God day and night, that He may uphold the cause of His servant and the cause of His people Israel according to each day's need, so that all the peoples of the earth may know that the Lord is God and that there is no other."

After that Solomon offered many sacrifices, and all the people held a feast with him. The people went home joyful and glad of heart, for all the good things the Lord had done for His servant David and His people Israel.

The Division of the Kingdom

1 Kings 11:1–12:24

At first Solomon was a good king. He trusted God and worshiped Him. But as Solomon grew older, he became proud, and he disobeyed God by marrying many foreign women and worshiping their idols with them. The Lord was angry with Solomon. He said to him, "Since this is your attitude and you have not kept My covenant and My decrees, . . . I will most certainly tear the kingdom away from you and give it to one of your subordinates. Nevertheless, for the sake of David your father, I will not do it during your lifetime. I will tear it out of the hand of your son."

Jeroboam was one of Solomon's officials. Because Jeroboam did his work well, Solomon gave him many duties.

One day, as Jeroboam went out of the city of Jerusalem, he met a prophet of God named Ahijah. Ahijah was wearing a new coat. When Ahijah saw Jeroboam, he took off his new coat and tore it into 12 pieces. Then he gave 10 pieces to Jeroboam. This was God's way of saying that the 12 tribes of Israel would be divided and that Jeroboam would rule over 10 of them.

Ahijah told Jeroboam, "This is what the Lord, the God of Israel, says: 'See, I am going to tear the kingdom out of Solomon's hand and give you 10 tribes. . . . I will give one tribe to his son so that David My servant may always have a lamp before Me in Jerusalem, the city where I chose to put My Name. . . . If you do whatever I command you and walk in My ways and do what is right in My eyes . . . , I will be with you. I will build you a dynasty as enduring as the one I built for David and will give Israel to you. I will humble David's descendants because of this, but not forever."

When Solomon heard what had happened, he wasn't sorry for his sins. He didn't ask God to forgive him. Instead, Solomon tried to put Jeroboam to death, but Jeroboam fled to Egypt and stayed there until Solomon's death.

When Solomon died, his son, Rehoboam, became king. Then Jeroboam returned from Egypt. Together with the whole assembly of Israel he went to Rehoboam.

"Your father put a heavy yoke on us, but now lighten the harsh labor and the heavy yoke he put on us, and we will serve you," the people said to Rehoboam.

Rehoboam wanted to think about this for a while. He asked the people to come back in three days. When the people left, Rehoboam went to the older men who served his father Solomon. He asked them how he should treat the people. The older men told Rehoboam to give the people a favorable answer, and they would always be his servants.

Next Rehoboam asked the younger men, who were about his own age. The young men told him to be rough and hard on the people.

Rehoboam decided to do what the young men said. So, when the people returned to Rehoboam, he told them that his father, Solomon, had been unkind to them but that he would treat them even more unkindly. Rehoboam thought the people would be afraid of him and would obey him if he spoke harshly to them. But most of the people wanted a different king.

So 10 of the 12 tribes of Israel left Rehoboam. They made Jeroboam their king, just as God had promised they would. Only a small part of the people followed Rehoboam as their king. Now, instead of one country, there were two countries: The kingdom of Judah with Rehoboam as king and the kingdom of Israel with Jeroboam as king.

Job

The Book of Job

Once there lived a man whose name was Job. Job was a good man who loved and followed God. Job had seven sons, three daughters, and great flocks and herds of sheep and cattle and camels and donkeys. Job also had many servants to look after all his possessions.

Job had a pleasant life until one day Satan came to see God.

"Where have you come from?" God asked Satan.

"From roaming through the earth and going back and forth in it," said Satan.

"Have you considered My servant Job?" asked God. "There is no one on earth like him; he is blameless and upright, a man who fears God and shuns evil."

"Does Job fear God for nothing?" replied Satan. "Have You not put a hedge around him and his household and everything he has? You have blessed the work of his hands, so that his flocks and herds are spread throughout the land. But stretch out Your hand and strike everything he has, and he will surely curse You to Your face."

"Very well, then," said God. "Everything he has is in your hands, but on the man himself do not lay a finger."

One day while his children were feasting a messenger came to Job.

"The oxen were plowing and the donkeys were grazing nearby, and the Sabeans attacked and carried them off. They put the servants to the sword, and I am the only one who has escaped to tell you!"

While he was still speaking, another messenger came running up.

"The fire of God fell from the sky and burned up the sheep and the servants," he said, "and I am the only one who has escaped to tell you!"

While he was still speaking, still another messenger appeared.

"The Chaldeans formed three raiding parties and swept down on your camels and carried them off," he said. "They put the servants to the sword, and I am the only one who has escaped to tell you!"

While he was still speaking, a fourth messenger arrived.

"Your sons and daughters were feasting and drinking wine…when suddenly a mighty wind swept in from the desert and struck the four corners of the house. It collapsed on them and they are dead," he said, "and I am the only one who has escaped to tell you!"

Job tore his clothes and shaved his head. Then he fell to the ground in worship and said, "Naked I came from my mother's womb and naked I will depart. The Lord gave and the Lord has taken away; may the name of the Lord be praised."

Then Satan went back to see God.

"Have you considered My servant Job?" God asked Satan. "There is no one on earth like him; he is blameless and upright, a man who fears God and shuns evil. And he still maintains his integrity, though you incited Me against him to ruin him without any reason."

"Skin for skin!" said Satan. "A man will give all he has for his own life. But stretch out your hand and strike his flesh and bones, and he will surely curse You to Your face."

"Very well, then," said God, "he is in your hands; but you must spare his life."

So Satan covered Job with terrible sores, from the soles of his feet to the top of his head.

"Are you still holding on to your integrity?" his wife asked. "Curse God and die!"

"You are talking like a foolish woman," said Job. "Shall we accept good from God, and not trouble?"

Now three of Job's friends came to visit him. They talked with him for a long time. And they all came to the same conclusion: God must be punishing Job because of something he did wrong.

But Job refused to listen to them. He knew God loved him and that one day He would save him.

Then a young man named Elihu came to see Job, and he also tried to explain why so many bad things had happened to Job.

Then God spoke to Job out of a storm. He told Job not to pay any attention to all the empty-headed words of those who had come to visit him. God said to Job, "I will question you, and you shall answer Me."

"I know that You can do all things; no plan of Yours can be thwarted," said Job.

Then God turned to Job's friends. "I am angry with you . . . because you have not spoken of Me what is right, as My servant Job has," He said. Job's friends offered sacrifices to God and Job prayed for them.

God made Job prosperous again. He gave him twice as many cattle and sheep and twice as much property as Satan had taken away from him. He blessed Job with seven more sons and three daughters and let him live to be 140 years old. Job lived to see four generations of his descendants before he finally died, an old man and full of years.

Psalms

The Book of Psalms

The book of Psalms was the prayer book and the songbook of the Hebrew people, the children of Israel. In the Psalms, God's people poured out their souls to Him. They also shouted wonderful songs of joy and sang great songs of thanksgiving and praise.

"Come, let us sing for joy to the Lord," the psalm writer wrote. "Let us shout aloud to the Rock of our salvation.

"Let us come before Him with thanksgiving and extol Him with music and song."

"Come, let us bow down in worship, let us kneel before the Lord our Maker, for He is our God and we are the people of His pasture, the flock under His care."

Many of the psalms are credited to King David. Others are credited to the "sons of Korah," to Solomon, and to Moses.

Listen to what King David prays in Psalm 16:

"Keep me safe, O God, for in You I take refuge.

"I said to the Lord, 'You are my Lord; apart from You I have no good thing.' . . .

"I will praise the Lord, who counsels me; even at night my heart instructs me.

"I have set the Lord always before me. Because He is at my right hand, I will not be shaken."

David was praying for safekeeping and thanking God for His protection and comfort.

In many ways the Psalms are a small version of all of the Old Testament. The book of Psalms points to God as the Creator and Ruler of all. It points to His justice and holiness. And it points to His Son, Jesus, as the Redeemer of His sinful children.

The Psalms reflect the faith of all of God's people. Today, too, we can sing with King David, "You have made known to me the path of life; You will fill me with joy in Your presence, with eternal pleasures at Your right hand."

Proverbs

The Book of Proverbs

The book of Proverbs teaches us about being wise, and it begins with something very wise indeed.

In the very first chapter of Proverbs, Solomon says, "The fear of the Lord is the beginning of knowledge."

And Solomon also says, "But fools despise wisdom and discipline."

Many of the proverbs in Proverbs are credited to King Solomon, who, because God gave him great wisdom, "spoke 3,000 proverbs and his songs numbered a thousand and five."

"A gentle answer turns away wrath," writes Solomon, "but a harsh word stirs up anger."

"The tongue that brings healing is a tree of life, but a deceitful tongue crushes the spirit."

Other proverbs were written by a wise man named Agur and a king named Lemuel.

"Speak up for those who cannot speak for themselves, for the rights of all who are destitute," says King Lemuel. "Speak up and judge fairly; defend the rights of the poor and needy."

Again and again the book of Proverbs points us to the true Source of wisdom: "Trust in the Lord with all your heart and lean not on your own understanding; in all your ways acknowledge Him, and He will make your paths straight."

Elijah and the Prophets of Baal

1 Kings 16:29–18:45

Many years after King David, King Solomon, and King Jeroboam had all died, a very wicked king named Ahab ruled the kingdom of Israel. He did more evil in the eyes of the Lord than any king before him. He and his wife, the wicked Queen Jezebel, worshiped idols called Baals and Asherahs instead of the true God. Jezebel killed many of God's prophets and teachers.

One day God sent a prophet to punish the king. The prophet's name was Elijah. Elijah came to the king and said, "As the Lord, the God of Israel, lives, whom I serve, there will be neither dew nor rain in the next few years except at my word." Then God told Elijah to hide in the Kerith Ravine, where King Ahab would not be able to find him.

Elijah obeyed. At the Kerith Ravine, God took care of Elijah. Every morning and evening ravens brought him bread and meat. And he drank water from the brook.

Some time later the brook dried up. Then God told Elijah to go to Zarephath, where God had commanded a widow to supply him with food. When he got to Zarephath, Elijah met a woman gathering sticks. When Elijah asked her to give him some food and water, she told him that she and her son had only enough food for one last meal. But Elijah told her, "Don't be afraid . . . . Make a small cake of bread for me . . . and then make something for yourself and your son. For this is what the Lord, the God of Israel, says: 'The jar of flour will not . . . run dry until the day the Lord gives rain on the land.' "

The woman obeyed, and Elijah's words were true. So there was food for Elijah and the woman and her son.

Some time later the woman's son became ill and died. Elijah took the widow's son from her arms and laid him on his bed. Stretching himself out on the boy three times, he prayed, "O Lord my God, let this boy's life return to him!" And the boy returned to life. Then the woman said to Elijah, "Now I know that you are a man of God and that the Word of the Lord from your mouth is true."

In a different way, God was taking care of the people of King Ahab too. By sending troubles to them He was working to lead them to be sorry for their sins so they would return to Him.

For three long years the people and the animals in Elijah's country suffered because there was no rain. Then God came to Elijah and said, "Go and present yourself to Ahab, and I will send rain on the land."

When King Ahab saw Elijah, he said, "Is that you, you troubler of Israel?"

Elijah said, "I have not made trouble for Israel, but you and your father's family have. You have abandoned the Lord's commands and have followed the Baals. Now summon the people from all over Israel to meet me on Mount Carmel. And bring the 450 prophets of Baal and the 400 prophets of Asherah, who eat at Jezebel's table."

So Ahab told all his priests and the people to come to Mount Carmel. There were 450 priests of the idol Baal, but Elijah was the only prophet of the true God left. Ahab had killed all the other prophets of God. Elijah went before the people and said, "How long will you waver between two opinions? If the Lord is God, follow Him; but if Baal is God, follow him." The people said nothing to Elijah.

Then Elijah told the people to build two altars and lay an offering on each with no fire under it. "Then you call on the name of your god," Elijah said, "and I will call on the name of the Lord. The god who answers by fire—he is God."

The people said to Elijah, "What you say is good."

The priests of the idol Baal had the first chance. They prayed and shouted all morning and afternoon and slashed themselves with swords and spears, thinking they could get their god's attention, but there was no answer, and no fire came. Toward evening Elijah told the people to come to his altar. Before Elijah prayed, he had some men pour water three times over the altar and the wood and the offering. Then Elijah prayed to God. "O Lord," prayed Elijah, ". . . let it be known today that You are God in Israel."

At once God sent fire from heaven. It burned the offering, the stones of the altar, and the wood lying on it. It even licked up the water in the ditch around the altar. When the people saw this, they knelt on the ground and said, "The Lord—He is God! The Lord—He is God!" Then Elijah told the people to catch all the wicked priests and put them to death.

Then God sent rain once again upon the land.

Naboth's Vineyard/Naaman and Elisha

1 Kings 21; 2 Kings 2:1–5:19

Naboth had a vineyard close to the palace of Ahab, king of Israel. And Ahab said to Naboth, "Let me have your vineyard to use for a vegetable garden, since it is close to my palace. In exchange I will give you a better vineyard or, if you prefer, I will pay you whatever it is worth."

But Naboth said, "The Lord forbid that I should give you the inheritance of my fathers."

And Ahab came into his house sullen and angry. He lay on his bed and sulking, refused to eat. But Jezebel, his wife, came to him and said, "Get up and eat! Cheer up. I'll get you the vineyard of Naboth."

So she wrote letters in Ahab's name and sent them to the elders and nobles, saying, "Proclaim a day of fasting and seat Naboth in a prominent place among the people. But seat two scoundrels opposite him and have them testify that he has cursed both God and the king. Then take him out and stone him to death." And the men did as Jezebel told them.

As soon as Jezebel heard that Naboth was dead, she said to Ahab, "Get up and take possession of the vineyard of Naboth . . . . He is no longer alive, but dead."

So the Lord said to Elijah, "Go down to meet Ahab . . . . He is now in Naboth's vineyard, where he has gone to take possession of it. Say to him, 'This is what the Lord says: Have you not murdered a man and seized his property? . . . In the place where dogs licked up Naboth's blood, dogs will lick up your blood. . . . Dogs will devour Jezebel by the wall of Jezreel. Dogs will eat those belonging to Ahab who die in the city, and the birds of the air will feed on those who die in the country.' "

And in the course of time all these things happened just as God had said. Later when Elijah's work on earth was done, God took him alive up to heaven, riding on a chariot of fire pulled in a whirlwind by horses of fire. To serve in Elijah's place, God chose the prophet Elisha.

In the days of Elisha a great man, named Naaman, lived in the land of Aram (Syria). He was captain of the king's army and had won many battles. But Naaman had leprosy. No doctor could heal him.

Some time earlier when the army of Aram had made war against God's people Israel, they had taken a little girl from her home and brought her to their own land. Here she became a servant to Naaman's wife.

One day the little girl said, "If only my master would see the prophet who is in Samaria! He would cure him of his leprosy." Naaman's wife told her husband what the girl had said.

When the king of Aram heard of it, he said: "By all means, go. I will send a letter to the king of Israel." So Naaman went to Israel, taking costly presents with him.

He also brought the letter to the king of Israel. When the king read the letter, he became afraid and did not know what to do. But Elisha heard what had happened. "Have the man come to me," he said.

So Naaman came with his horses and chariots and stopped at the door of Elisha's house.

But Elisha did not come out to see Naaman. Instead, he sent a messenger to tell him, "Go, wash yourself seven times in the Jordan, and your flesh will be restored and you will be cleansed."

This made Naaman angry. He thought the prophet should come out and pray to his God and heal him. He turned around and went away.

But his servants said to him, "If the prophet had told you to do some great thing, would you not have done it?" So Naaman went down and dipped himself in the Jordan River seven times. When he came out of the water, he was healed.

At once Naaman went back to Elisha's house. He said to the prophet: "Now I know that there is no God in all the world except in Israel." He wanted to give Elisha the presents, but Elisha would not take anything. "Go in peace," he said to the captain. So Naaman went home with a glad heart.

Jeremiah's Call/The Fall of Jerusalem

The Book of Jeremiah

As a young boy Jeremiah was sure he would be a priest at the temple in Jerusalem. His father, you see, was a priest. That is why Jeremiah was so surprised one day when God came to him and said he should be a prophet. "I do not know how to speak," said Jeremiah. "I am only a child."

God touched Jeremiah's mouth and said, "I have put My words in your mouth. Do not be terrified . . . , for I am with you."

So Jeremiah became a prophet of God. He began to tell the people of Judah that God did not like their idolatry. But the people did not want Jeremiah to talk about their sins. Instead of becoming sorry for their sins and asking God to forgive them, they became angry with Jeremiah. They wouldn't even let him come into the temple anymore.

One day God said to Jeremiah, "Take a scroll and write on it all the words I have spoken to you . . . . Perhaps when the people of Judah hear about every disaster I plan to inflict on them, each of them will turn from his wicked way; then I will forgive their wickedness and their sin."

Jeremiah asked his friend Baruch to help write down all that God had said. Then, because he wasn't allowed in the temple himself, he had Baruch read the words to the people in the temple.

One day one of the leaders of the people heard these words that Jeremiah wrote. He was worried because he knew the words were true. He told the other leaders, and they decided that they must tell the king.

Now, the leaders knew that King Jehoiakim would be very angry to hear the words of Jeremiah. So they told Jeremiah and his friend to hide. Then they took the scroll to the king.

All the leaders gathered round the king, and it was commanded that the words of Jeremiah should be read. The king was sitting in front of a fire. As the words were read, the king cut apart, bit by bit, the scroll Baruch had written, and threw God's words into the fire. The leaders begged the king not to do this, but he wouldn't listen.

The king ordered his servants to arrest Jeremiah and Baruch. He was very angry. And he was not sorry for his sins. But the servants of the king couldn't find Jeremiah or Baruch because God had hid them.

Later God told Jeremiah to write the same words on another scroll. So, even though he burned them, the king could not destroy God's words. And at last God's words came true: Nebuchadnezzar, a mighty foreign king, came and took Jehoiakim, who had burned God's Word, and put him in prison. Nebuchadnezzar also carried the people of Judah and Jerusalem away from the land God had given them and into his own country, Babylon, where they lived in captivity.

The Three Men in the Fiery Furnace/ Daniel in the Lion's Den

Daniel 3, 6

King Nebuchadnezzar of Babylon did not believe in the true God. He prayed to idols.

King Nebuchadnezzar made an image of gold 90 feet high and 9 feet wide. He ordered that all the people should fall down and pray to the image when they heard the sound of music. But there were three men from Judah who prayed only to the true God. They were Shadrach, Meshach, and Abednego.

When the king heard that they would not fall down and pray to the image, he became very angry. He called the three and said, "Now when you hear the sound of the horn, flute, zither, lyre, harp, pipes and all kinds of music, if you are ready to fall down and worship the image I made, very good. But if you do not worship it, you will be thrown immediately into a blazing furnace. Then what god will be able to rescue you from my hand?"

The three men answered, "If we are thrown into the blazing furnace, the God we serve is able to save us from it, and He will rescue us from your hand, O king. But even if He does not, we want you to know, O king, that we will not serve your gods or worship the image of gold you have set up."

This answer made the king still more angry. He told the people to make the furnace seven times hotter than at other times.

He sent his strongest soldiers to tie these three men and to throw them into the furnace. It was so hot that the heat killed the soldiers who threw Shadrach, Meshach, and Abednego into the fire.

Soon the king began to be amazed, for when he looked into the furnace, he did not see three men but four! They were not tied! They were walking around untied in the fire! And they were not burned! The fourth man was an angel. God had sent him to keep Shadrach, Meshach, and Abednego from being hurt by the fire.

The king called to the three brave men. "Shadrach, Meshach, and Abednego, servants of the Most High God, come out! Come here!" The three men came out of the fire. They were not burned. Not even their hair had caught fire, and there was no smell of smoke on their clothes.

The king said, "Praise be to the God of Shadrach, Meshach, and Abednego, who has sent His angel and rescued His servants! They trusted in Him and defied the king's command and were willing to give up their lives rather than serve or worship any god except their own God." King Nebuchadnezzar made a law that any man who said anything against the true God should be put to death. Then he made Shadrach, Meshach, and Abednego some of his highest officers.

After Nebuchadnezzar died, Belshazzar became king of Babylon. One night soon after Belshazzar had become king, the armies of the Medes and Persians broke into the city of Babylon and captured it. They killed Belshazzar and put Darius on the throne.

Darius was quick to realize that he needed help to rule his large kingdom; therefore he appointed 120 satraps to take charge of the various provinces. Over the satraps the king set three administrators, one of whom was Daniel, a friend of Sahadrach, Meshach, and Abednego.

Since Daniel was good and wise, the king made him the chief of the administrators, and he had in mind putting him in charge of the entire kingdom.

When the satraps and other leaders saw how much Darius favored Daniel, they became envious and began to look for a way to make trouble for him. They watched Daniel carefully, hoping to find some fault with his work. But they found no fault of any kind.

Then the satraps and other leaders held a meeting. They agreed that the only place in which they could hope to make Daniel seem guilty of breaking a law was in his religion. They went to the king and said, "O King Darius, live forever! The royal administrators, prefects, satraps, advisers and governors have all agreed that the king should issue an edict and enforce the decree that anyone who prays to any god or man during the next 30 days, except to you, O king, shall be thrown into the lions' den. Now, O king, issue the decree and put it in writing so that it cannot be altered—in accordance with the laws of the Medes and Persians, which cannot be repealed."

The king saw no harm in such a law. And because he had no idea of what was behind the request, he made the law and signed it.

Daniel was not present when the new law was made, but he soon heard about it. Nevertheless he knelt down before the window of his house that opened toward Jerusalem and prayed to God three times each day, as he had always done.

The envious officials watched secretly. They saw Daniel praying at his window. At last they had a way of getting Daniel into trouble.

They hurried to the king and said, "Did you not publish a decree that during the next 30 days anyone who prays to any god or man except to you, O king, would be thrown into the lions' den?"

The king said yes, he had.

Then the officials said, "Daniel, who is one of the exiles from Judah, pays no attention to you, O king, or to the decree you put in writing. He still prays three times a day."

When Darius heard this, he was angry with himself for letting envious officials deceive him into signing a foolish law. Poor Daniel, he thought. Was there a way to save him? The law could not be changed. Till sundown the king tried to think of a way of getting around the law, but he found none. There was nothing left to do but give the order to throw Daniel into the lions' den. Quickly some servants carried out the order.

The king's last words to Daniel were, "May your God, whom you serve continually, rescue you."

The door to the den was closed with a large stone. The king put his seal on the stone, so no one would dare to move it.

Sorrowfully Darius returned to his palace. All that night he found it impossible to sleep.

As soon as daybreak came, the king hurried to the lions' den. In a trembling voice he called out, "Daniel, servant of the living God, has your God, whom you serve continually, been able to rescue you from the lions?"

Daniel answered, "My God sent His angel, and he shut the mouths of the lions. They have not hurt me."

Darius was glad when he heard this. At his command Daniel was taken out of the den. The king was angry with the men who had deceived him and plotted the death of Daniel. He ordered his servants to throw them, as well as their families, into the lions' den. The hungry lions sprang up at the men and their families as they fell and broke their bones before they reached the floor of the den.

After this the king made a new law. In it he commanded all his people to respect the God of Daniel, the living God, who had saved him from the power of the lions.

Daniel prospered under King Darius, and also under King Cyrus, who succeeded Darius on the throne.

Jonah

The Book of Jonah

Long ago there was a prophet whose name was Jonah. God told Jonah to preach to a great city called Nineveh. Jonah did not want to go. Instead, he went to the sea and tried to run away by getting on a ship that was sailing far away from Nineveh. But God was watching him.

As the ship was sailing along, God sent a violent storm. The ship was about to break into pieces. The sailors threw out all of the goods to make the ship lighter, but the storm grew worse. Then every sailor prayed to his god for help. Still the storm kept on.

All this time Jonah was sleeping down below in the ship. The captain came to him and said: "How can you sleep? Get up and call on your god! Maybe he will take notice of us, and we will not perish."

122

The sailors thought that someone on the ship might have done a great wrong. They cast lots to find out who it could be, and the lot fell on Jonah.

Now Jonah had to tell them what he had done. He told them, "Pick me up and throw me into the sea, and it will become calm." The sailors did not want to do this, but the storm grew worse.

At last they took Jonah and threw him into the sea. Then the wind stopped blowing right away. When the sailors saw this, they feared the God of Jonah and offered sacrifices to Him.

God did not forget about Jonah. He sent a big fish to where Jonah was thrown into the sea, and this fish swallowed Jonah whole.

For three days and three nights Jonah was in this fish. There he thought about his sins and began to pray to God. Then God spoke to the fish, and the fish came near the shore and spit Jonah up on dry land.

Once more God told Jonah to go to Nineveh. This time Jonah went. Nineveh was a very big city, and its people were very wicked. When Jonah came into the city, he began to preach. "Forty more days and Nineveh will be overturned," he said.

The people and the king believed Jonah's message was from God and were sorry for having sinned. They prayed to the God of Jonah and brought sacrifices, hoping that He would have mercy on them. When God saw what they did and how they turned from their evil ways, He had compassion and did not bring upon them the destruction He had threatened.

But Jonah was greatly displeased at God's mercy toward Nineveh. "I knew that You are a gracious and compassionate God, slow to anger and abounding in love, a God who relents from sending calamity," he said.

Jonah was so angry at God that he wanted to die. He went out of the city to watch and see if anything would happen to Nineveh. While he waited, God provided a vine that grew up over Jonah to give shade for him, and Jonah was very happy about the vine. But early the next day God sent a worm, which chewed the vine so that it withered. And once again, Jonah grew so angry he wanted to die.

And God said to Jonah, "Do you have a right to be angry about the vine? . . . You did not tend it or make it grow. It sprang up overnight and died overnight. But Nineveh has more than 120,000 people . . . . Should I not be concerned about that great city?"

Caesarea Philippi

Mediterranean Sea

GALILEE

Capernaum

Sea
of
Galilee

Cana

Nazareth

Jordan River

SAMARIA

Jericho

Mount of Olives

Jerusalem
Bethany

JUDEA

Bethlehem

Dead Sea

The New Testament

John Prepares the Way (Part 1)

Luke 1:5–25, 57–80

Before Jesus was born there lived in Judea a priest, Zechariah, and his wife, Elizabeth. This godly couple was well along in years. But they had no children.

Zechariah was taking his turn serving at the temple, burning incense, when an angel of the Lord appeared to him. Zechariah was frightened at the sight of the angel. But the angel said, "Do not be afraid, Zechariah; your prayer has been heard. Your wife Elizabeth will bear you a son, and you are to give him the name John."

Zechariah asked, "How can I be sure of this? I am an old man and my wife is well along in years."

"I am Gabriel," the angel said. "I have been sent to speak to you and to tell you this good news. And now you will be silent and not able to speak until the day this happens, because you did not believe my words."

Gabriel's words came true. When Zechariah left the temple, he was not able to speak.

Elizabeth was very happy when she knew that God was going to give her a son in her old age. "The Lord has done this for me," she said. ". . . He has shown His favor."

When Elizabeth became the mother of a baby boy, not only she and Zechariah, but also their neighbors and relatives shared their joy.

On the eighth day after his birth the baby was to be given a name. All the friends thought Zechariah and Elizabeth were going to call him Zechariah, after his father.

But Elizabeth said, "No! He is to be called John." The neighbors were surprised and said, "There is no one among your relatives who has that name."

Then the neighbors asked Zechariah to tell everyone what name the baby should have. Zechariah had them bring him a slate, and he wrote on the slate, "His name is John." Immediately Zechariah was able to speak again. At once he began to praise God. All the people were much surprised. They wondered what the baby would be when he grew up.

When John grew up, he became a preacher. He preached to the people. He told them to turn away from their sins and to wait for the Savior.

John said the Savior would come soon. The Savior would teach them and save them from their sins. John also baptized all who were sorry for their sins and believed in the promised Savior.

Because he baptized the people, he is called John the Baptist.

127

The Annunciation

Matthew 1:18–24, Luke 1:26–56

Beautifully situated among the hills of southern Galilee was a quiet little city called Nazareth, where there lived a God-fearing young woman named Mary. Mary was engaged to be married to a carpenter named Joseph.

One day about six months after the angel Gabriel had appeared to Zechariah, God had sent the angel to Mary to bring her some wonderful news. "Greetings, you who are highly favored!" the angel said. "The Lord is with you!"

Mary wondered what this greeting might mean. But the angel said, "Do not be afraid, Mary, you have found favor with God. You will be with child and give birth to a son, and you are to give Him the name Jesus. He will be great and will be called the Son of the Most High. The Lord God will give Him the throne of His father David, and . . . His kingdom will never end."

Mary wondered how this could be, as she was not married. But Gabriel said, "The Holy Spirit will come upon you, and the power of the Most High will overshadow you. So the Holy One to be born will be called the Son of God. Even Elizabeth your relative is going to have a child in her old age, . . . For nothing is impossible with God."

After Mary had heard this, she said, "I am the Lord's servant. May it be done to me as you have said."

Then the angel left her.

The news Mary had received was too wonderful to keep to herself. Quickly she got ready and hurried to the place where Zechariah and Elizabeth lived. As soon as Mary entered her relatives' house and greeted them, Elizabeth's baby leaped in her womb and Elizabeth exclaimed, "Blessed are you among women, and blessed is the child you will bear! But why am I so favored, that the mother of my Lord should come to me? Blessed is she who has believed that what the Lord has said to her will be accomplished!"

Mary was so happy that from deep in her soul there came the words of a beautiful hymn of praise. "My soul glorifies the Lord," she said, "and my spirit rejoices in God my Savior, for He has been mindful of the humble state of His servant. From now on all generations will call me blessed, for the Mighty One has done great things for me—holy is His name! His mercy extends to those who fear Him, from generation to generation."

After visiting with Elizabeth about three months, Mary returned to her home.

When Joseph learned that Mary would become a mother, he was troubled. But being a godly man, he did not want to disgrace Mary; so he decided to set aside their marriage agreement in a private way. But this was not pleasing to God. To change Joseph's mind, God had an angel appear to him in a dream and say, "Do not be afraid to take Mary home as your wife, because what is conceived in her is from the Holy Spirit. She will give birth to a son, and you are to give Him the name Jesus, because He will save His people from their sins."

All this happened to fulfill the prophecy the Lord made through the prophet Isaiah when he said, "The virgin will be with child and will give birth to a son, and they will call Him Immanuel—which means, 'God with us.' "

After the angel had spoken to Joseph, he took Mary to his home as his wife.

Jesus Is Born

Luke 2:1–20

There came a time in the reign of Roman ruler Augustus when he made a new tax law. It said that all the people in the Roman Empire should be listed, or registered, for taxing. In the land of Palestine the people had to be registered in the city or village in which their ancestors had lived.

The new tax law was put to use for the first time when a man named Quirinius governed the province of Syria, which was near Palestine. Soon after the new law was made known, large numbers of people were on the move. All were going to the place where they were supposed to register. Joseph, the carpenter of Nazareth, also started on his way. Although Mary, his wife, was soon to have a child, she went with him. Since both Mary and Joseph were descendants of King David, they had to travel from their home in Nazareth 70 miles south to the city of David, which was Bethlehem.

Bethlehem was a small town. When Mary and Joseph arrived there, they found it crowded with people. It was so crowded that they could not find a room in which to stay. Finally they took shelter in a stable, where cattle were kept.

While Mary and Joseph were in Bethlehem, to be listed for taxing, the time came for the child to be born whose coming the prophets of the Old Testament had foretold. This was the child whose coming the angel of the Lord had announced to Mary—the promised Messiah.

Thus it was that in the middle of the night in a stable in Bethlehem Mary gave birth to Jesus, the Son of God and Savior of the world. He was her first child. She wrapped Him in strips of cloth and laid Him in a manger.

Nearby in the fields were shepherds watching their sheep. At once an angel appeared, shining the glory of the Lord on them. The shepherds were terrified. But the angel said, "Do not be afraid. I bring you good news of great joy that will be for all people. Today in the

town of David a Savior has been born to you; He is Christ the Lord.
This will be a sign to you: You will find a baby wrapped in cloths and
lying in a manger."

Then suddenly a great number of angels appeared with the first
angel. They praised God saying, "Glory to God in the highest, and on
earth peace to men on whom His favor rests."

After the angels left, the shepherds said, "Let's go to Bethlehem
and see this thing that has happened, which the Lord has told us
about."

So they lost no time. Quickly they went to Bethlehem and found
Mary, Joseph, and the baby Jesus.

After they saw Jesus, they spread the word about the birth of the
Savior and all who heard it were amazed. When the shepherds
returned to their work, they did so praising and thanking God for all
the wonderful things they had heard and seen.

Mary pondered all these events and treasured their memory.

The Coming of the Magi

Matthew 2:1–12

After Jesus was born God put a very special star into the sky. Some Wise Men (Magi) who lived far away in the east saw the star, and followed it for many days until they came to Jerusalem.

Here they asked, "Where is the one who has been born king of the Jews. We saw His star in the east and have come to worship Him." But no one could tell them where the new king was.

An evil king lived in Jerusalem. His name was Herod. When he heard that a new king had been born, he became worried that someone wanted to be king in his place.

Herod asked some teachers where Jesus was to be born. "In Bethlehem," they said.

Then Herod called the Wise Men and said, "Go and make a careful search for the child. As soon as you find Him, report to me, so that I too may go and worship Him."

Herod did not tell the truth when he said this. He really wanted to kill Jesus.

The Wise Men started on their way to Bethlehem. They were glad when they saw the star again. It went before them and stood over the house where Jesus was.

There the Wise Men went into the house and found Jesus. They were very happy. Worshiping Jesus, they knelt down before Him. Then they opened their treasures and gave Him gifts of gold, incense, and myrrh.

Then they were ready to go home. Before they started on their way, God warned them in a dream not to go back to Herod, so they went home by another route.

133

Jesus in the Temple

Luke 2:41–52

Every year in the springtime the people of the land where Jesus lived held a great festival at the temple in Jerusalem. The festival lasted for seven days, and they called it the Passover.

At this festival God's people thanked Him for the wonderful way in which He had brought them out of Egypt many, many years before.

Large crowds went to Jerusalem and to the beautiful temple for the celebration. Mary and Joseph lived far away in Nazareth, but every year they went, too.

When 12-year-old Jesus was in Jerusalem celebrating the Passover with His family, Mary and Joseph had started for home, unknowingly leaving Him behind. At the end of the first day of their journey, Mary and Joseph discovered Jesus was missing. When they did not find Him with friends and relatives, they went back to Jerusalem to look for Him there.

After three days they found Jesus in the temple. He was sitting among some Bible teachers, listening to them and asking them questions. All who heard Jesus were surprised at how well He knew the Bible.

Mary said to Jesus, "Son, why have You treated us like this? Your father and I have been anxiously searching for You."

Jesus said to His mother, "Why were you searching for Me? Didn't you know that I had to be in My Father's house?"

Then Jesus went home with His parents and obeyed them. He grew every day; He learned His lessons well; He obeyed God's commandments; and people loved Him.

God the heavenly Father loved Him, too.

John Prepares the Way (Part 2)

Luke 3:1–18

When John the Baptist grew up, he went into the country around the Jordan River, preaching a baptism of repentance for the forgiveness of sins. As Isaiah the prophet had predicted, John was the voice calling in the desert to prepare the way for the Lord. Isaiah had foretold John's coming many years before.

John told the people about Jesus. Concerned about how to prepare for the coming Savior, the people asked, "What should we do then?"

John answered, "The man with two tunics should share with him who has none, and the one who has food should do the same."

Tax collectors also came to be baptized. "Teacher," they asked, "what should we do?"

"Don't collect any more than you are required to," he told them.

Then some soldiers asked him, "And what should we do?"

He replied, "Don't extort money and don't accuse people falsely—be content with your pay."

As the people waited for the coming of the Savior, they wondered if John might possibly be the Christ.

But John answered them all, "I baptize you with water. But one more powerful than I will come, the thongs of whose sandals I am not worthy to untie. He will baptize you with the Holy Spirit and with fire." And so John continued to preach to the people, telling them to repent and then comforting them with the good news of Jesus the Savior.

Jesus Is Baptized/Jesus Is Tempted in the Wilderness

Matthew 3:1–17, 4:1–11

One day Jesus came to John the Baptist at the Jordan River to be baptized by him.

But John resisted. It did not seem proper to John that a sinful person like himself should baptize someone who had no sin. John said to Jesus, "I need to be baptized by You, and do You come to me?"

Jesus said to John, "Let it be done so now; it is proper for us to do this to fulfill all righteousness."

Then John stepped with Jesus into the Jordan and baptized Him.

137

As soon as the baptism was over, Jesus came out of the water. Then a wonderful thing happened. The heavens opened, and the

Spirit of God came down in the form of a dove and alighted on Jesus. At the same time a voice from heaven said, "This is My Son, whom I love; with Him I am well pleased."

It was the voice of the heavenly Father. He was pleased with His Son because He willingly offered Himself to do all that needed to be done to save everyone from the everlasting punishment of sin.

After this, the Spirit of God led Jesus into the desert to be tempted by the devil. Jesus stayed there 40 days and 40 nights. During this time He ate nothing, and so He became desperately hungry.

Knowing that Jesus was very hungry, the devil said, "If you are the Son of God, tell these stones to become bread."

Jesus did not give in to the devil. Responding with words from Scripture He said, "It is written, 'Man does not live on bread alone, but on every word that comes from the mouth of God.' "

Having failed in his first attempt to lead Jesus into sin, Satan tried again. He took Jesus to Jerusalem and had Him stand on the highest part of the temple. "If You are the Son of God," he said, "throw Yourself down. For it is written, 'He will command His angels concerning you, and they will lift you up in their hands, so that you will not strike your foot against a stone.' "

This sounded very proper, but the devil did not quote the Bible correctly. He should have said that God will order His angels to protect a person when he is doing what pleases God. Putting oneself unnecessarily into danger to see if He will send help is not pleasing to God. He does not want to be tested in this way; therefore Jesus said to Satan, "It is also written, 'Do not put the Lord your God to the test.' "

Again Satan was defeated, but he tried a third time to get Jesus to sin. This time he took Jesus to the top of a high mountain, and in a moment he showed Him the kingdoms of the world and all the riches and glory of them. Boldly he said to Jesus, "All this I will give You if You will bow down and worship me."

How very wicked of Satan to ask Jesus to worship him!

Jesus said, "Away from Me, Satan! For it is written: 'Worship the Lord your God and serve Him only.' "

Then the devil left Jesus, and the angels came and worshiped Jesus.

Jesus Calls His Disciples

John 1:29–51; Luke 5:27–31; 6:12–16

One day, while John the Baptist was talking with two of his disciples, Jesus came walking by. Seeing Him, John pointed to Jesus and said to his disciples, "Look, the Lamb of God, who takes away the sin of the world!"

As soon as the two disciples, Andrew and John, heard this, they left John the Baptist and followed Jesus. Like many other people, they too had been waiting for the coming of the Savior. Now John pointed Him out to them, and they were eager to get acquainted with Him.

When Jesus had walked on a little way, He turned, saw the two men behind Him, and He began talking with them.

"Where are you staying?" they asked Jesus.

"Come and you will see," He replied.

Andrew and John went with Jesus and spent the rest of the day with Him. Both Andrew and John believed that Jesus was the promised Savior, and they became His disciples.

John the Baptist did not mind losing disciples to Jesus, for he knew that it was his business to lead people to the Savior.

Now Andrew had a brother named Simon. When Andrew found Jesus, he was so glad that he could hardly wait until he could tell his brother about Him. So he began to search for Simon. As soon as Andrew found him, he said, "We have found the Messiah."

Then he brought Simon to Jesus. When Jesus saw Simon, He gave him a new name. He called him Peter, a name that means "rock."

The next day Jesus found Philip and said to him, "Follow Me." Philip then found Nathanael and told him, "We have found the one Moses wrote about in the Law and about whom the prophets also wrote—Jesus of Nazareth, the son of Joseph."

"Nazareth! Can anything good come from there?" Nathanael asked.

"Come and see," said Philip.

When Jesus met Nathanael He said, "I saw you while you were still under the fig tree before Philip called you."

Marveling that Jesus knew Nathanael was sitting under a fig tree when Philip called him, Nathanael confessed, "You are the Son of God; You are the King of Israel."

But Jesus said, "You believe because I told you I saw you under the fig tree. You shall see greater things than that. . . . You shall see heaven open, and the angels of God ascending and descending on the Son of Man."

Later Jesus went up to a tax collector named Levi, sitting at his tax booth. "Follow Me," Jesus said. And Levi got up, left everything and followed Him. Then Levi held a great banquet for Jesus at his house. Levi invited a large crowd of tax collectors. But the Pharisees and teachers of the Law criticized Jesus' disciples for eating and drinking with tax collectors and "sinners." But Jesus said, "It is not the healthy who need a doctor, but the sick. I have not come to call the righteous, but sinners to repentance."

In addition to Andrew, John, Peter, Philip, Nathanael (also called Bartholomew), and Levi (also called Matthew), Jesus chose James, Thomas, James son of Alphaeus, Simon the Zealot, Judas son of James, and Judas Iscariot to be His disciples.

Jesus Gives the Sermon on the Mount

Matthew 5–7

Jesus was on His way up a mountainside. His disciples and a large number of other people followed Him.

When Jesus came to a suitable place, He sat down. Then the crowd spread out before Him, and He began to preach a sermon. It has come to be known as the Sermon on the Mount. In this sermon Jesus explained the commandments of God and told how people who believe in Him will live. He began by speaking of the blessedness, or happiness, of His children.

Happy are the people, Jesus said, who know they are sinful and think they are not good enough to have God's favor, for the kingdom of heaven belongs to them.

Happy are the people who are sorrowful and sad because they have disobeyed God, for He will forgive them and make them joyful.

Happy are the people who are eager to obey God, for He will lead them to do the things that please Him.

Happy are the people who are merciful and help others, for they will receive mercy and help.

Happy are the people whose hearts are pure, for they shall see God and live with Him forever.

Happy are the people who keep peace and make peace where there is quarreling, for they will be known as children of God.

Happy are the people who are laughed at and mistreated because they love and serve the Lord, for the kingdom of heaven belongs to them.

Jesus continued His sermon by telling how He wants His children to live. They are to set a good example by living godly lives, speaking the truth and loving God and all people—including their enemies. Instead of finding fault with others, they are to guard against doing evil themselves. They are not to kill anyone, or even be angry with others. Instead of getting revenge when someone has harmed them, they are to forgive and return good for evil. At all times

141

they are to treat others the way they want to be treated themselves.

The first concern of God's children will not be the hoarding of money and other earthly goods. They will rather be concerned about glorifying God and living with Him in heaven.

In speaking about prayer, Jesus said that we should not make a show of our praying by doing it in public places, hoping that people will see us and praise us for our goodness. Neither should we pray like those who say many meaningless words, thinking that their prayers will be heard because they have done much talking.

After this Jesus taught the Lord's Prayer. He also promised that the heavenly Father would surely hear the prayers of His children.

Jesus told the people not to worry. Toward the end of the sermon Jesus warned His children to be on guard against false teachers of religion. They appear to be teachers of the truth, He said, but they really lead people away from God instead of to God.

Last of all Jesus said that the mere hearing of His Word is not enough. It must also be obeyed. Those who hear His Word and obey it are like the wise man who built his house on a rock—a solid foundation. As the house was firm against winds and floods and rain, so the people who put their trust in Christ, the Rock, will be firm when troubles and temptations come. Those, however, who hear God's Word and do not obey it are like the foolish man who built his house on sand. When troubles and temptations come, they will lose their faith and life with God forever.

The people who heard the sermon were astonished at the power with which Jesus taught, for He spoke like one who had the right to teach and whose words were the truth.

We need not wonder that the people were astonished, for Jesus was the greatest of all teachers. He was the Teacher whom God had sent—the Son of God. Through faith in Him we live a life blessed by God.

Jesus Changes Water into Wine

John 2:1–11

A few days after Jesus had gathered the first of His disciples, He went to a wedding. This wedding was in a small town called Cana, in Galilee.

Mary, the mother of Jesus, was at the wedding. Many other people were there, too, including Jesus' disciples.

Wine was served, but there was not enough for all the people. Soon it was all used up. Mary knew about the trouble. She went to Jesus for help. She said, "They have no more wine."

Jesus said to His mother, "My time has not yet come."

Mary believed that Jesus would help. So she went to the servants and said, "Do whatever He tells you."

Six large water jars stood nearby. Jesus said to the servants, "Fill the jars with water." So they filled them to the brim.

Jesus now said to them, "Now draw some out and take it to the master of the banquet."

When the servants did as Jesus told them, they saw that Jesus had done a wonderful miracle. He had changed water into wine!

The man in charge of the feast tasted the new wine and found that it was very good. He did not know where it had come from.

He called the bridegroom aside and said, "Everyone brings out the choice wine first . . . but you have saved the best till now."

Changing water into wine was the first miracle that Jesus did. By this miracle He proved that He is the Son of God, and His disciples believed in Him.

Nicodemus

John 3

One night a Pharisee, a ruler of the people, came to Jesus. His name was Nicodemus. He had heard about the miracles Jesus had done. He was sure that Jesus must be a very wise and a very great man. He wanted to talk to Jesus.

Nicodemus said to Jesus, "Rabbi, we know You are a teacher who has come from God. For no one could perform the miraculous signs You are doing if God were not with Him."

Jesus knew that Nicodemus had come to learn about living with God in His kingdom. "I tell you the truth," said Jesus, "no one can see the kingdom of God unless he is born again."

At first Nicodemus could not understand what Jesus meant. He said, "How can a man be born when he is old?" Jesus answered, "I tell you the truth, no one can enter the kingdom of God unless he is born of water and the Spirit."

Jesus meant that only those who have their sins washed away and receive God's Spirit become His children and live with Him in His kingdom.

Nicodemus still was puzzled. He said, "How can this be?" Jesus answered, "You are Israel's teacher and you do not understand these things? . . . We speak of what we know. Just as Moses lifted up the snake in the desert, so the Son of Man must be lifted up, that everyone who believes in Him may have eternal life."

Jesus was telling how He would suffer and die on the cross so that all people could have forgiveness of sins and eternal life.

Then He said the best-known words in the Bible: "For God so loved the world that He gave His one and only Son, that whoever believes in Him shall not perish but have eternal life."

People become children of God when the Holy Spirit gives them faith in Jesus, their Savior, who died for them. God's children live with Him both now and forever.

Jesus and the Samaritans

John 4:1–42

Generally, Jewish people hated Samaritans. They wanted nothing to do with them because the Samaritans had descended from a mixture of Israelite people and the people of several foreign nations. Besides, they had a false religion.

But Jesus loved the Samaritans the same as other people, and He wanted to save them from their sin, too.

One day Jesus and His disciples came to a well in Samaria outside the city of Sychar. Here Jesus sat down to rest while the disciples went into the city to buy food. Soon a Samaritan woman from Sychar came to the well to get water. Jesus wanted to save her from her sin; so He spoke to her. He asked for a drink of water. The woman said to Jesus, "You are a Jew and I am a Samaritan woman. How can You ask me for a drink?"

Jesus answered, "If you knew the gift of God and who it is that asks you for a drink, you would have asked Him and He would have given you living water."

Living water? The woman did not know what Jesus meant. She said, "Sir, You have nothing to draw with and the well is deep. Where can You get this living water?"

Then Jesus explained the difference between "living water" and ordinary water, such as was in the well. He said, "Everyone who drinks this water will be thirsty again, but whoever drinks the water I give him will never thirst. Indeed the water I give him will become in him a spring of water welling up to eternal life."

"Sir," the woman said, "Give me this water so that I won't get thirsty and have to keep coming here to draw water."

Jesus wanted to make the woman realize that she was lost in sin and that she needed the kind of water of which He had spoken— God's love and forgiveness. Jesus told her about the wicked things she had done—things she thought nobody knew. Jesus said, "Go, call your husband."

"I have no husband," replied the woman.

"You are right," Jesus said, ". . . The fact is, you have had five husbands, and the man you now have is not your husband."

"I can see that You are a prophet," said the woman. "Our fathers worshiped on this mountain, but you Jews claim that the place where we must worship is in Jerusalem."

Jesus responded by saying that the place in which one worships is not important. The God one worships, and how one worships Him—that's important. The true God—God the Father, God the Son, and God the Holy Spirit—who made Himself known to the Israelites, is the one who must be worshiped, and He must be worshiped with a heart filled with faith in Him.

Now the woman realized that she was a sinner and that she needed the Messiah, the promised Savior. "When He comes," she said, "He will explain everything to us."

Then Jesus declared, "I, who speak to you, am He."

Just then the disciples returned from the city. They were astonished when they saw their master talking with a Samaritan woman, but they asked no questions about it.

How happy and excited the woman must have been. She left her water jar at the well and rushed off to Sychar to spread the glad news. "Come, see a man who told me everything I ever did. Could this be the Christ?"

Many Samaritans believed Jesus was the Christ because of what the woman said about Him. And a large number of Samaritans went out to Jesus. They invited Him to stay with them and Jesus stayed two days. During this time He taught about God's love and forgiveness. Then many more Samaritans believed. "We know that this man really is the Savior of the world," they said.

Jesus Heals the Official's Son

John 4:43–53

Once while Jesus was visiting in Cana in Galilee, where He had turned the water into wine, the son of a royal official was lying sick at Capernaum.

When this man heard that Jesus had arrived from Judea, he went to Jesus as quickly as he could to pray for his son, for he was close to death.

Jesus said, "Unless you people see miraculous signs and wonders, you will never believe."

The father prayed again, saying, "Sir, come down before my child dies."

Then Jesus spoke kindly to the man. He said, "You may go. Your son will live."

Trusting Jesus' words the man began his journey home. While still on his way, some servants met him with the news that his son was better.

The father asked what time his son began to improve. The servants answered, "The fever left him yesterday at the seventh hour [one o'clock]."

The father remembered that one o'clock was exactly the time when Jesus had said, "Your son will live."

As a result of this miracle, the father, son, and everyone else in their household came to believe in Jesus as the Son of God and the only Savior of the world.

Jesus Heals the Man at the Bethesda Pool

John 5:1–18

In the great city of Jerusalem was a pool called Bethesda. Around the pool were five porches, and on them lay many people who were sick or blind or lame.

At certain times the water would bubble. The sick people would then step into the water. They believed that whoever stepped in first after the water had bubbled became well.

150

One day Jesus came to Jerusalem and went by the pool of Bethesda. He saw a man lying there who had been an invalid for 38 years. Jesus went up to him and said, "Do you want to get well?" The man looked up at Jesus and answered, "Sir, I have no one to help me into the pool when the water is stirred. While I am trying to get in, someone else goes down ahead of me."

Jesus felt sorry for the man. He said, "Get up! Pick up your mat and walk." At once the man became perfectly well. He got up, took the mat upon which he had been lying, and began to walk.

As the happy man walked around, carrying the mat, the leaders of the people saw him. "It is the Sabbath," they said to him; "the law forbids you to carry your mat."

The leaders had a strict rule against doing any work on the Sabbath day. But the man replied, "The man who made me well said to me, 'Pick up your mat and walk.' "

"Who is this fellow," they asked, "who told you to pick it up and walk'?" But the man who had been made well did not know because Jesus had disappeared into the crowd.

Later, however, Jesus found the man in the temple. Jesus said to him, "You are well again. Stop sinning, or something worse may happen to you."

Now the man knew it was Jesus who had cured him. He went and told the leaders that it was Jesus who had made him well.

Because Jesus had done these things on a Sabbath day, the leaders of the people thought He had disobeyed God's law, and they were angry with Him.

But Jesus said to them, "My Father is always at His work to this very day, and I, too, am working."

That made the leaders still more angry, because Jesus called God His own Father and in so doing called Himself God.

Peter's Great Catch of Fish

Luke 5:1–11

One day Jesus was teaching near the Sea of Galilee. So many people crowded around Him that it was hard for Jesus to speak.

Some fishermen had brought their boats close to shore and left them while they washed their nets. Jesus stepped into one of the boats, which belonged to Simon Peter, and asked him to push it out a little from the land. Then Jesus sat down in the boat and taught the people from the boat.

After the sermon, Jesus said to Simon, "Put out into deep water, and let down the nets for a catch." Simon answered, "Master, we've worked hard all night and haven't caught anything. But because You say so, I will let down the nets."

When the fishermen let down the nets into the water, they caught so many fish that the nets began to tear. They waved to their partners in the other boat to come and help them pull up the nets.

They now filled both boats so full of fish that the boats began to sink.

When Simon Peter saw the miracle, he fell down at Jesus' knees and said, "Go away from me, Lord; I am a sinful man."

The miracle showed that Jesus is the almighty Son of God, and Peter felt that he was too sinful to be near Jesus. But Jesus said to Peter, "Don't be afraid; from now on you will catch men."

Jesus meant that Peter and his partners would be missionaries who would tell many people of the Savior and His love. So they pulled their boats up on shore, left everything, and followed Jesus.

Jesus Heals the Man Sick with the Palsy

Luke 5:17–26

In a city called Capernaum there lived a very sick man. He could not move, so he had to lie helpless in bed.

One day some friends told him that Jesus was in Capernaum. The sick man believed that Jesus could help him. He wanted to go to Jesus.

So his friends laid him on a mat and carried him to the house where Jesus was teaching the people. But when they got there, they found the house so crowded with people that they could not get in.

The friends knew what to do. They carried the sick man up an outside stairway to the roof. They made a hole in the roof, tied ropes to the mat, and let the man down into the house through the hole.

Now the man was right in front of Jesus. Jesus knew he was sorry that he had sinned, so He said to him, "Friend, your sins are forgiven."

But the Pharisees and teachers of the Law began to think to themselves, "Who is this fellow . . . ? Who can forgive sins but God alone?"

Jesus knew what they were thinking, so He said, "Which is easier: to say, 'Your sins are forgiven,' or to say, 'Get up and walk'? But that you may know that the Son of Man has authority on earth to forgive sins . . ." Now Jesus said to the man, "Get up, take your mat and go home."

As soon as Jesus had said this, the man got up. He picked up his mat and went home. Thankful and happy, he praised Jesus for forgiving his sins and making him well.

Then everyone praised God. They said, "We have seen remarkable things today."

Jesus Raises the Dead

Luke 8:40–56

One day while Jesus was teaching, Jairus, a ruler of a synagogue, fell at Jesus' feet. He pleaded with Jesus to come to his house because his only daughter, a girl of about 12, was dying.

As Jesus was on His way the crowds gathered around Him. And a woman who had been bleeding for 12 years came up and touched Jesus' cloak. Immediately her bleeding stopped.

When Jesus asked who touched Him, the woman fell at His feet, trembling. In the presence of all the people she told why she had touched Jesus and how she had been instantly healed.

Jesus said to her, "Your faith has healed you. Go in peace."

155

While Jesus was still speaking, a man came from Jairus' house and said to him, "Your daughter is dead. Don't bother the teacher any more."

But Jesus said to Jairus, "Don't be afraid, just believe, and she will be healed."

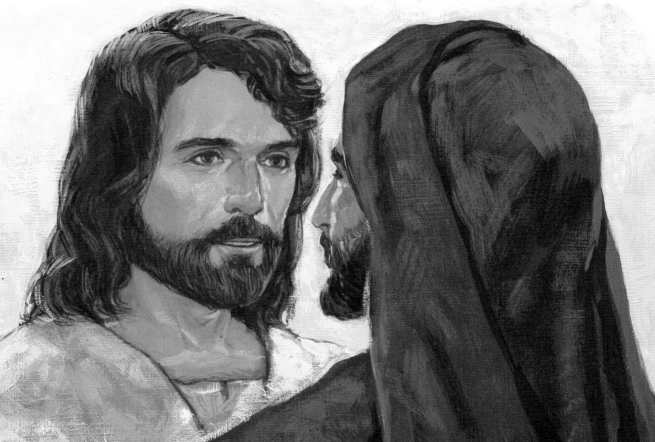

When they came to the house, they found it filled with people.

Women were crying and weeping, and men were playing funeral music. Jesus said to them, "Stop wailing. She is not dead but asleep."

The people thought it was foolish to say the girl was asleep. They knew she was dead. So they laughed at Jesus. Jesus told them all to leave the house.

He went with the father and the mother and Peter, James, and John into the room where their dead daughter lay. He took her by the hand and said, "My child, get up!"

At once the girl got up. Jesus had made the girl alive again. Her parents were astonished.

Jesus Stills the Storm

Matthew 8:23–27; 10:29–31

Jesus was near the Sea of Galilee. All day He was busy teaching a large crowd of people and healing those who were sick. But, in the evening, He sent the people away.

Then He and His disciples got into a boat and started across the sea. Jesus lay down in the back part of the boat and fell asleep. He was very tired.

Soon, without warning, a storm came up. The wind blew harder and harder. High waves splashed water into the ship. The disciples were afraid. They thought they would surely drown. They came to awaken Jesus and cried, "Lord, save us! We're going to drown!"

Jesus awoke, and He said to them, "You of little faith, why are you so afraid?" Then He stood up and spoke to the wind, and it became completely calm. The disciples were amazed at Jesus. "Even the winds and the waves obey Him!" they said.

Why had the disciples been afraid? They had forgotten that Jesus is the almighty Son of God, that He loves His children dearly and will help them in every trouble.

Sometime later Jesus taught His disciples about fear. He wanted them to know they need never be afraid. "Are not two sparrows sold for a penny?" Jesus asked. "Yet not one of them will fall to the ground apart from the will of your Father. And even the very hairs of your head are all numbered. So don't be afraid," Jesus reminded them. "You are worth more than many sparrows."

Jesus and the Gerasenes

Matthew 8:28–34; Mark 5:1–20; Luke 8:26–39

The morning after Jesus stilled the storm on the Sea of Galilee, He and His disciples came to shore in the country of the Gerasenes. There two men came running and screaming toward Him. Both of these men had evil spirits that had taken complete control over them. Because of the evil spirits, the men went about naked and lived in caves that had been used as burial places. They were so fierce that it was dangerous to travel through the area in which they lived, and they were so strong that it was impossible to control them. Several attempts had been made to chain the men, but each time they snapped the chains. So they were free to do as they pleased.

Speaking for himself and for his companion, one of the men said, "What do you want with us, Son of God? Have You come here to torture us before the appointed time?"

Jesus asked the man, "What is your name?"

A demon inside the man made him say, "Legion."

The word *legion* means "many." The man meant to say that he had the name Legion because many demons lived in him.

The evil spirits, knowing that their time for torturing the two men was at an end, begged Jesus to permit them to enter a herd of hogs grazing quietly on a hillside near the lake. Jesus gave them this permission. Immediately the evil spirits came out of the men, entered the hogs, and made the whole herd dash madly down the steep hillside and into the lake, where all of them drowned.

When the men in charge of the hogs saw this, they hurried away and reported what happened. Soon a large crowd went out to see things for themselves. As they approached Jesus, they noticed that the two men who had been tortured by evil spirits were sitting quietly beside Him. The men were clothed now, and each was in his right mind.

The people became afraid of Jesus, and they asked Him to leave. Jesus did what the people asked. He went to the boat to start on

His way back across the lake. But before the boat sailed away, one of the men who had been healed came and begged Jesus for permission to go with Him. He wanted to show Jesus how thankful he was. But Jesus did not allow the man to go along. It was far more important for him to show his thanks in another way; therefore Jesus said to him, "Return home and tell how much God has done for you."

The man did as he was told. In his city and in the towns round about he declared that Jesus had healed him. All who heard him were greatly amazed.

Jesus Teaches about His Kingdom

Matthew 13:1–30, 36–43

Jesus often taught people by telling them stories. One day Jesus told the story of a man who sowed some seed. He said:

"A farmer went out to sow his seed." Like all farmers in Jesus' day, this man did not have tractors and other farm equipment. Instead, he planted the seed by throwing handfuls over the ground as he walked back and forth.

Some of the seed fell on a path where the ground was hard. It couldn't start growing. Soon birds came and picked it up. In another part of the field the ground was not very deep. Rocks were near the top of it. The seeds that fell on this ground started to grow. But when the sun became hot, the little plants died because the roots could not find enough water and food.

Some seed fell among thorns. When the thorns grew up, they choked the little plants that had started to grow. The man didn't get any food from those plants either.

But some of the seed fell on good ground. It came up and grew, and soon each plant was filled with good grain. Some of the seed grew into 30 more seeds, some made 60, and some plants had even 100 new seeds on them.

After Jesus had told this story, His disciples asked Him what it meant.

Jesus explained that the seed is the Word of God and that the sower is like all those who teach God's Word. Those who hear the Word of God are the ground in which the seed is planted.

Some who hear what God says in the Bible are like the hard ground on the path. They do not understand what they hear. So the Word of God cannot even begin growing in their hearts. They soon forget what they hear.

Some of those who hear God's Word are like the rocky ground. They gladly listen and believe for a while. But when they have trouble, they stop doing what God wants them to do.

There are also people who are like the ground with thorns. Instead of believing and loving God, they worry and think about making money and having a good time, and God's Word cannot grow in their hearts.

But the good ground is like those who listen to God's Word and, by the power of the Holy Spirit, come to believe it. They do the things God wants His children to do, and the seed grows into strong faith and a godly life.

Then Jesus told another story. This story was about a farmer who planted good seed in his wheat field. During the night an enemy of the farmer came and sowed weeds in the farmer's field, because he wanted to ruin the farmer's work.

So the weeds planted by the enemy grew up alongside the farmer's wheat. When the farmer's servants saw the weeds, they asked the farmer, "Do you want us to go and pull them up?"

"No," the farmer replied, " . . . Let both grow together until the harvest. At that time I will tell the harvesters: First collect the weeds and tie them in bundles to be burned; then gather the wheat and bring it into my barn."

With this story Jesus taught about His second coming. On that day all who are evil will be destroyed like the weeds collected by the servants and burned at the harvest. But all who trust in Jesus for salvation He will keep close to Himself like the grain gathered and carefully stored by the farmer in his barn.

Jesus Feeds the Hungry

John 6:1–15

Jesus wanted to rest, so He took His disciples to a lonely place across the Sea of Galilee. But the people saw where they were going and followed them.

Jesus felt sorry for the people. He taught them and healed the sick. Then He went up the side of a hill and sat down with His disciples.

Soon they could see thousands of people coming up to them. Jesus said to Philip, "Where shall we buy bread for these people to eat?"

162

Jesus already had in mind what He was going to do. He wanted to see if Philip would trust in Him to feed the people. But Philip answered: "Eight months' wages would not buy enough bread for each one to have a bite!"

Then Andrew, Simon Peter's brother, spoke up, "Here is a boy with five small barley loaves and two small fish, but how far will they go among so many?"

Jesus said, "Have the people to sit down." There was plenty of grass in that place and about 5,000 men sat down, besides women and children.

When they were seated, Jesus took the five loaves and the two fish and thanked God. Then He gave the food to the disciples and the disciples gave it to the people. Everyone had as much as he or she wanted and there was enough for all of them.

When all had eaten, Jesus said to His disciples, "Gather the pieces that are left over. Let nothing be wasted." The disciples filled 12 baskets full of leftover barley loaves.

When the people saw the miracle Jesus had done, they wanted to force Him to be their king. But Jesus went up to a mountain to be by Himself for a time.

163

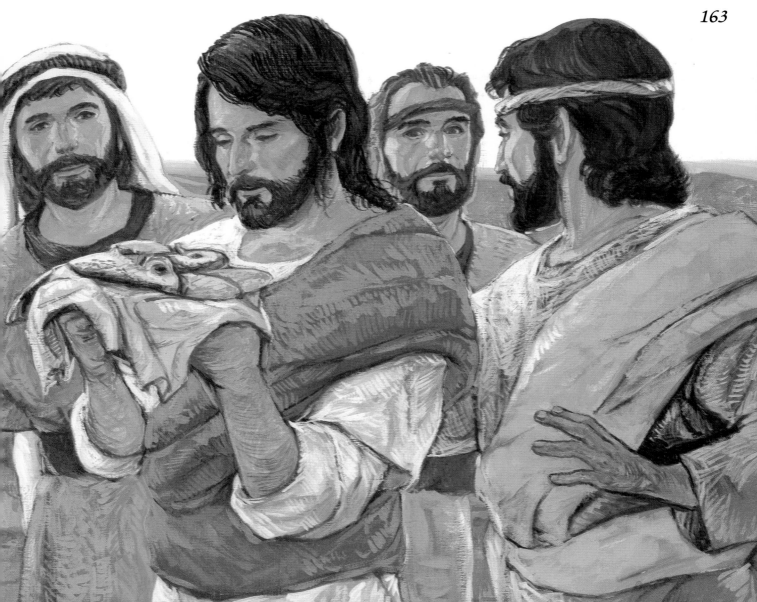

Jesus Walks on Water

John 6:16–21; Matthew 14:22–33

While Jesus was alone on the mountain, talking to His heavenly Father in prayer, evening came and His disciples went down to the lake, got into a boat, and set off across the lake for Capernaum. When it was dark a storm came up. The wind blew hard and the waters grew rough.

The disciples had to row with all their might, as the wind was against them.

About three o'clock that morning the disciples saw something moving on the water. It was coming toward their boat. At first the disciples thought it was a ghost and cried out in fear.

But it was Jesus, who was coming to His disciples in a wonderful way. He was walking on the water just as we walk on land.

"Take courage! It is I. Don't be afraid," called Jesus.

Hearing these words, Peter said, "Lord, if it's You, tell me to come to You on the water."

Jesus said: "Come."

So Peter began to walk toward Jesus on the water.

But before Peter reached Jesus, he saw a big wave coming toward him, and he became afraid. At once he began to sink, and he cried out, "Lord, save me!"

Quickly Jesus stretched out His hand, caught Peter, and said to him, "You of little faith, why did you doubt?"

As Jesus and Peter stepped into the boat, the winds stopped. Those who were in the boat were very much surprised at the wonderful power of Jesus.

They worshiped Him, saying, "Truly You are the Son of God!"

Peter's Confession/ The Transfiguration

Matthew 16:13–27; 17:1–9; Luke 9:28–36

"Who do people say the Son of Man is?"

This is the question Jesus asked His disciples when they were on their way to the district of Caesarea Philippi north of the Sea of Galilee.

The disciples answered, "Some say John the Baptist, others say Elijah; still others, Jeremiah or one of the prophets."

Then Jesus asked His disciples this very important question: "Who do you say I am?"

Peter answered for all the disciples. Boldly and firmly he said, "You are the Christ, the Son of the living God."

Jesus said to Peter, "Blessed are you, Simon son of Jonah, for this was not revealed to you by man, but by My Father in heaven."

Next Jesus told His disciples about the sorrows and troubles that would soon come to Him in Jerusalem. There the elders, the chief priests, and the scribes would treat Him cruelly and finally put Him to death. But on the third day after His death, He would rise alive from His grave.

Jesus said this so that His disciples would realize what a tremendous price He would have to pay to obtain forgiveness of sin for all people.

But Peter took Jesus aside and said to Him, "Never, Lord! This shall never happen to You!"

Peter meant well, but he was interfering with the will of God; therefore Jesus rebuked him sharply. He told Peter to get out of His sight, for in urging Him not to suffer and die, Peter was speaking for Satan, who did not want Jesus to do what needed to be done to save the world from sin.

After this Jesus gathered the disciples and other people around Him and explained what it meant to be one of His followers. He talked about what is most important. He said that a true follower turns away from sin and puts Jesus first in his or her life, suffering whatever pain and trouble may come because he or she is a follower. A follower trusts completely in Jesus as the only Savior from sin.

The time would come, Jesus continued, when He would return to the earth in glory, attended by His holy angels. Then He would judge all people according to what they had done. All who lived as true followers would be received into heaven. But all who proved by the way they lived that they were not true followers would be sent into everlasting punishment.

After six days Jesus and three of His disciples, Peter, James, and his brother John, climbed up a high mountain. When they reached the top, Jesus spoke to His heavenly Father in prayer.

While He was praying, a wonderful thing happened. His face became as bright as the sun and His clothes dazzling white. Thus, covered with heavenly light, Jesus appeared like the glorious Son of God that He was.

Two men suddenly stood with Jesus. One was Moses, and the other was Elijah. They, too, appeared in heavenly glory. Both of these men had been received into heaven many years before, but now they were sent to speak with Jesus about His suffering and death, which would take place in Jerusalem.

Although the three disciples were very sleepy, they managed to keep awake enough to see Jesus and the men with Him in heavenly glory. This glory filled the hearts of the disciples with a strange fear. At the same time they were overjoyed by what they saw. It seemed so good that they hoped it could continue a long time. This led Peter to say to Jesus, "Master, it is good for us to be here. Let us put up three shelters—one for You, one for Moses and one for Elijah."

Peter meant well when he mentioned it, but he was so overcome with joy that he did not quite know what he was saying; so Jesus did not answer him.

While Peter was still speaking, a bright cloud came and covered all who were there. From the cloud the voice of God came, saying, "This is My Son, whom I have chosen; listen to Him."

Upon hearing this, the disciples fell on their faces, for they were afraid. But Jesus came, touched them, and said, "Get up. Don't be afraid."

When the disciples got up and looked around, they saw that the cloud was gone, that Moses and Elijah were gone, and that the heavenly glory was gone. Everything had returned to the way it was in the first place.

The next day Jesus and the three disciples started down the mountain. On the way down Jesus ordered them not to tell anyone what happened on the mountain until He had risen from the dead. For if the news of it had been spread around, the people of the land would have been strengthened in their mistaken idea that Jesus had come into the world to free them from the rule of the Roman government, instead of as their Savior from sin. The disciples obeyed their Lord. They kept silent at that time, telling no one anything of what they had seen.

Jesus Heals the Man Born Blind

John 9:1–38

On a certain Sabbath after Jesus and His disciples had left the temple and were walking through the streets of Jerusalem they met a beggar who was born blind.

When the disciples noticed this man they began to wonder why he was born blind. Like many other people, they thought that misfortunes came as punishment for some particular sin. They said to Jesus, "Rabbi, who sinned, this man or his parents, that he was born blind?"

"Neither this man nor his parents sinned," Jesus said, "but this happened so that the work of God might be displayed in his life."

As Jesus said this, He made a bit of mud by moistening some clay with His saliva. He spread the mud on the man's eyelids and then said, "Go, wash in the Pool of Siloam."

The blind man made his way to the pool and washed the mud from his eyes. At that moment a miracle happened, for when the man walked away, he could see.

Filled with joy, he hurried home. When the people saw him going about and doing things like those who can see, there was much excitement among them. It was hard for them to believe that this was the same man who had been born blind. They asked, "Isn't this the same man who used to sit and beg?"

Some were quite sure he was the same man, but others disagreed. "No," they said, "he only looks like him."

At last the one who had been born blind settled the matter, saying, "I am the man."

When he was asked how his eyes came to be healed, he told everything that Jesus had done. And in reply to the question as to where Jesus was, he said he didn't know. Then some of the neighbors took the man who had been blind to the Pharisees. They did this because they were tattlers who wanted Jesus to be blamed for healing the man on the Sabbath. The Pharisees wanted to know how the man got his sight. When he told them how Jesus had healed him, some of the Pharisees said that Jesus had disobeyed God by healing on the Sabbath.

But others disagreed. They said, "How can a sinner do such miraculous signs?"

Next the Pharisees conducted an investigation into the healing. They questioned the man who had been born blind, they questioned his parents, and then they questioned him again.

Finally the man said this about Jesus, "Whether He is a sinner or not, I don't know. One thing I do know. I was blind, but now I can see!"

After that the Pharisees insulted the man and threw him out of the synagogue.

170

When Jesus heard what had happened, He looked up the man who had been blind. When He found him, He said, "Do you believe in the Son of Man?"

The man who had been blind answered by saying, "Who is He, sir?" the man asked. "Tell me so that I may believe in Him."

"You have now seen Him," Jesus said, "in fact, He is the one speaking with you."

Then the man joyfully cried out, "Lord, I believe," and he worshiped Him.

The Good Samaritan

Luke 10:29–37

"Who is my neighbor?" a lawyer once asked Jesus. To answer the question, Jesus told this story.

A certain man was going from Jerusalem to Jericho. On the way some robbers stopped him, tore off his clothing, and beat him until he was nearly dead.

Then they ran away, leaving the poor man on the roadside.

After a while a priest happened to come that way. He saw the wounded man, but did not stop to help him. Instead, he hurried by on the other side of the road.

Soon another man came along. This man was a Levite. He worked in the temple and was supposed to be a very holy person. The Levite, too, saw the wounded man, but did not help him. Like the priest, he passed by on the other side of the road.

At last a Samaritan came the same way. He looked at the wounded man and went to the man and helped him. He cleaned his wounds and put bandages on them. Then he put the man on his donkey and brought him to an inn. There he took care of him.

The next day the Samaritan had to travel farther. Before he went away, he gave some money to the innkeeper and said: "Look after him, and when I return, I will reimburse you for any extra expense you may have."

This is the story that Jesus told. After the story He said to the lawyer, "Which of these three do you think was a neighbor to the man who fell into the hands of robbers?"

The lawyer answered, "The one who had mercy on him."

Then Jesus said, "Go and do likewise."

Jesus wants us to be kind to everyone.

Mary and Martha

Luke 10:38–42

Jesus often went up to Jerusalem to teach and to be at the services in the temple. On His journeys He liked to stay in the quiet little town of Bethany, which was near Jerusalem.

Here lived some good friends of Jesus—the sisters Mary and Martha and their brother Lazarus.

One day Jesus came to Bethany, and Martha invited Him to her home. Jesus was pleased to come, and the sisters knew it was a great honor to have Jesus as their guest.

When Jesus came to their house, He sat down to teach. Mary sat down at the feet of Jesus and listened closely to every word He spoke.

While Mary sat there listening, Martha was running back and forth, very much excited about the meal. She loved Jesus just as Mary did, and she thought the best way to honor the Lord was to make a good supper for Him.

Martha was displeased because Mary did not come and help her. She went to Jesus and said, "Lord, don't You care that my sister has left me to do the work by myself? Tell her to help me."

Jesus looked at Martha in His friendly way and said, "Martha, Martha, you are worried and upset about many things, but only one thing is needed. Mary has chosen what is better, and it will not be taken away from her."

The best thing for all of us is first to hear the word of Jesus and then do our work.

Jesus, the Good Shepherd

John 10:1–18

Many of the people who came to hear Jesus teach made their living by caring for sheep. As Jesus taught these people many of them became sorry for their sins, so Jesus wanted them to know about God's love, forgiveness, and salvation. These are the gifts Jesus came to bring us through His life, death, and resurrection from the dead.

In order to tell them these spiritual truths in a way they would understand, Jesus compared the people to sheep; and He compared Himself to the gate of the pen that the sheep entered in order to be safe.

"I tell you the truth . . . ," Jesus said. "I am the gate; whoever enters through Me will be saved. He will come in and go out and find pasture."

Warning against false teachers Jesus compared them to thieves. "The thief comes only to steal and kill and destroy," said Jesus. But then He added, "I have come that they may have life, and have it to the full."

Speaking of His love for all people, Jesus said, "I am the good shepherd, I know My sheep and My sheep know Me—just as the Father knows Me and I know the Father—and I lay down My life for the sheep."

Jesus wanted the people to know that He would have followers from all parts of the world, so He said, "I have other sheep that are not of this pen. I must bring them also. They too will listen to My voice, and there shall be one flock and one shepherd."

Our loving shepherd willingly gave up His life for us. Trusting in Him we need have no worries. Jesus gave everything, even His very life, for us. He will guard and guide us through life, faithfully leading us to our happy home in heaven.

The Foolish Rich Man

Luke 12:13–31

"Teacher, tell my brother to divide the inheritance with me."

With these words some rude fellow who could think of nothing but money once interrupted Jesus while He was busy teaching.

Jesus refused to settle the quarrel between the brothers, for that was the business of the courts, so He said, "Man, who appointed Me a judge or an arbiter between you?"

Then Jesus turned to the crowd and said, "Watch out! Be on your guard against all kinds of greed; a man's life does not consist in the abundance of his possessions."

To impress His warning against greed, Jesus told a parable. He said:

"The ground of a certain rich man produced a good crop. He though to himself, 'What shall I do? I have no place to store my crops.'

Then he said, 'This is what I'll do. I will tear down my barns and build bigger ones, and there I will store all my grain and my goods. And I'll say to myself, 'You have plenty of good things laid up for many years. Take life easy; eat, drink and be merry.' "

All the man's thinking was about his well-being in the future years. But he wasn't going to have any future years. God said to him, "You fool! This very night your life will be demanded from you. Then who will get what you have prepared for yourself?"

With these words Jesus ended His parable. But He went on instructing the people. He said, "This is how it will be with anyone who stores up things for himself but is not rich toward God."

Jesus continued His teaching by saying to His disciples, "Do not worry about your life, what you will eat; or about your body, and what you will wear. Consider the ravens: They do not sow or reap, they have no storeroom or barn; yet God feeds them. And how much more valuable you are than birds! Who of you by worrying can add a single hour to his life? Since you cannot do this very little thing, why do you worry about the rest?

"Consider how the lilies grow. They do not labor or spin. Yet I tell you, not even Solomon in all his splendor was dressed like one of these. If that is how God clothes the grass of the field, which is here today, and tomorrow is thrown into the fire, how much more will He clothe you, O you of little faith! And do not set your heart on what you will eat or drink; do not worry about it. For the pagan world runs after all such things, and your Father knows that you need them. But seek first His kingdom, and these things will be given to you as well."

The Lost Son

Luke 15:11–24

One day some people were surprised to see Jesus talking with sinners. To show that He is ready to forgive sinners who are sorry for their sins, Jesus told a story about a man who had two sons. One day the younger son said to his father, "Father, give me my share of the estate." So the father gave the young man everything that would one day belong to him.

A few days later the young man gathered all that was his and went far away from home. There he wasted his money in sinful pleasure, and soon it was all gone.

Then a great famine came into the land, and the young man had nothing to eat. Now he had to work for his living, but work was hard to find.

At last a man living there hired him to take care of his pigs. The young man was so hungry that he wished to eat the food that was given to the pigs.

One day he began to think how foolish he had been. He said to himself, "How many of my father's hired men have food to spare, and here I am starving to death! I will set out and go back to my father and say to him: 'Father, I have sinned against heaven and against you. I am no longer worthy to be called your son; make me like one of your hired men.' "

At once the young man started on his way home. When he was still far down the road, his father saw him coming, and filled with love for his son, he ran out to meet him. He put his arms around him and kissed him.

The son said, "Father, I have sinned against heaven and against you. I am no longer worthy to be called your son."

But the father said to his servants, "Quick! Bring the best robe and put it on him. Put a ring on his finger and sandals on his feet. Bring the fattened calf and kill it. Let's have a feast and celebrate. For this son of mine was dead and is alive again; he was lost and is found." So they began to celebrate.

Like the father in the story, God is ready and glad to receive anyone who is sorry for his or her sins and turns back to Him.

179

The Rich Man and Lazarus

Luke 16:19–31

One day Jesus told a story about two men. One was a rich man. The rich man dressed in fine clothes, ate rich and fancy delicacies, and lived every day in luxury. By contrast, at his gate was a beggar, named Lazarus. Lazarus was covered with sores. The dogs came and licked Lazarus' sores, and he longed to eat the scraps from the rich man's table.

Eventually, the beggar died. The angels carried him to heaven, where he lived in the company of Abraham.

The rich man also died and was buried. In hell he looked up and, being in torment, saw Abraham far away with Lazarus by his side. So he called out, "Father Abraham, have pity on me and send Lazarus to dip the tip of his finger in water and cool my tongue, because I am in agony in this fire."

But Abraham said, "Son, remember that in your lifetime you received your good things, while Lazarus received bad things, but now he is comforted here and you are in agony. And besides all this, between us and you a great chasm has been fixed, so that those who want to go from here to you cannot, nor can anyone cross over from there to us."

Then the rich man said, "Then I beg you, father, send Lazarus to my father's house, for I have five brothers. Let him warn them, so that they will not also come to this place of torment."

Abraham responded, "They have Moses and the Prophets; let them listen to them."

"No, Father Abraham," the rich man said, "but if someone from the dead goes to them, they will repent."

And he said to him, "If they do not listen to Moses and the Prophets, they will not be convinced even if someone rises from the dead."

The Raising of Lazarus

John 11:1–45

Mary and Martha were good friends of Jesus. They lived in Bethany, near Jerusalem, with their brother, Lazarus. One day Lazarus became very sick. So Mary and Martha sent someone to Jesus with the message that Lazarus was very sick.

When Jesus heard the news, He said, "This sickness will not end in death. No, it is for God's glory so that God's Son may be glorified through it." Now Jesus loved Mary and Martha and Lazarus, but still He stayed two more days in the place where He was.

After that Jesus said to His disciples, "Our friend Lazarus has fallen asleep; but I am going there to wake him up."

At first the disciples thought that Lazarus was only asleep and that soon he would wake up. Then Jesus said, "Lazarus is dead."

When Jesus came to Bethany, Lazarus had been in the grave four days. Martha said, "Lord, if You had been here, my brother would not have died."

Then Jesus said, "Your brother will rise again." Martha said, "I know he will rise again in the resurrection at the last day."

Jesus said, "I am the resurrection and the life. He who believes in Me will live, even though he dies; and whoever lives and believes in Me will never die." Jesus now asked Martha, "Do you believe this?"

Martha answered, "Yes, Lord, I believe that You are the Christ, the Son of God."

Now when Mary also came out to meet Jesus, they went to the grave of Lazarus. Many people had come to comfort Mary and Martha. All of them were weeping. Jesus also wept.

The grave was like a cave, and a big stone had been put in front of the opening. Jesus said to the men, "Take away the stone." Then He looked up to heaven and prayed aloud.

After that He said with a loud voice, "Lazarus, come out!" And Lazarus, who had been dead four days, came out of the grave and was alive again.

When the people saw this great miracle, many of them believed that Jesus surely must be the Son of God.

The 10 Lepers

Luke 17:11–19

Jesus was going into a village when He met 10 men with leprosy.

Lepers were not allowed to live in towns or to come near other people because of their dreadful sickness. So the 10 men stood there by themselves, away from the people.

But at a distance they cried out, "Jesus, Master, have pity on us!" These men believed that Jesus could make them well, just as He had made many other sick persons well.

Jesus saw the 10 sick men. He also heard them begging for help. But He did not make them well at once. "Go, show yourselves to the priests," He said.

If lepers got over their sickness, the priests were to look at them. The priests were to say whether they were cured. If they were cured, they could live with other people again.

The lepers obeyed Jesus, even though He did not make them well at once. They started on the road to Jerusalem to show themselves to the priests in the temple.

As they were walking along, they found that the sickness had left them. Jesus had answered their prayer and made them well.

One of the 10 men turned back at once and praised God with a loud voice. He came to Jesus, fell down at His feet, and thanked Him. This man was a Samaritan.

Jesus looked at the Samaritan. "Were not all 10 cleaned?" He asked. "Where are the other 9? Was no one found to return and give praise to God except this foreigner?"

Then Jesus said to him, "Rise and go; your faith has made you well."

The Pharisee and the Tax Collector

Luke 18:9–14

In the crowd that followed Jesus on His last journey to Jerusalem there were people who were much like the Pharisees. They believed they had lived perfect lives and therefore were free from sin.

Pleased with themselves and with their supposed goodness, they looked down on other people. To their way of thinking, they alone were people of real importance.

To make these people see themselves as they really were, proud and lost in sin, Jesus told a parable about two men who went into the temple to pray. One was a Pharisee; the other a publican, or tax collector.

The Pharisee, wanting to be seen by the people in the temple, stood well up in front when he prayed. Since he had no knowledge of his sin, he did not repent or ask to be forgiven. Instead he told God what a good man he was. He said, "God, I thank You that I am not like other men—robbers, evildoers, adulterers—or even like this tax collector. I fast twice a week and I give a tenth of all I get."

When the tax collector prayed, he stood far in the rear, where he would not attract attention. Well he knew how wicked he had been and how unworthy he was of God's help. He could not get himself to lift up his eyes toward heaven when he prayed. He felt too sorrowful and ashamed for that. In deep grief over his wickedness he struck his breast, confessed his sin, and humbly asked to be forgiven. He said, "God, have mercy on me, a sinner."

Since the tax collector repented of his sin and trusted in God's mercy, God forgave him and declared him to be free from sin and the punishment of sin. Thus he went home a righteous man. But the Pharisee, who did not repent of his sin or long for the mercy of God, went home unforgiven.

That is what Jesus meant when He spoke the following about the tax collector to those who were listening: "I tell you that this man, rather than the other, went home justified before God. For everyone who exalts himself will be humbled, and he who humbles himself will be exalted."

The Rich Young Ruler

Matthew 19:16–26

One day a rich young man came up to Jesus to ask Him a question. This young man was in charge of a synagogue, the house of worship, and he was rich.

Falling at the feet of Jesus, the young man asked, "Teacher, what good thing must I do to get eternal life?"

Jesus said, "If you want to enter eternal life, obey the commandments."

"Which ones?" asked the young man.

Jesus answered, "Do not murder, do not commit adultery, do not steal, do not give false testimony, honor your father and mother, and love your neighbor as yourself."

The young man was pleased when he heard this. He said, "All these I have kept. What do I still lack?"

184

Jesus loved the young man and felt sorry for him. He saw that money was dearer to him than God.

So Jesus said, "If you want to be perfect, go sell your possessions and give to the poor, and you will have treasure in heaven. Then come, follow Me."

When the young man heard this, he walked away sad, for he loved his money and did not want to give it away.

As Jesus watched him go, He said, "I tell you the truth, it is hard for a rich man to enter the kingdom of heaven. Again I tell you, it is easier for a camel to go through the eye of a needle than for a rich man to enter the kingdom of God."

Surprised at Jesus' words, the disciples asked Him, "Who then can be saved?"

Jesus looked at them and said, "With man this is impossible, but with God all things are possible."

Zacchaeus

Luke 19:1–9

In Jericho there lived a man whose name was Zacchaeus. He was a chief tax collector and he was wealthy. You may remember that tax collectors often collected more than was right and kept the extra money. That is why the people hated them and called them great sinners.

One day Jesus was passing through Jericho. When Zacchaeus heard that Jesus was in his city, he wanted very much to see Him.

So he hurried out and joined the crowd that was following Jesus. However, when Zacchaeus came to the place where Jesus was, he could not see Him because he was too short to see over the heads of the crowd.

But Zacchaeus had an idea. He ran ahead of the crowd and climbed up a tree. There he waited for Jesus to pass by. When Jesus came to the tree, He stopped and looking at Zacchaeus, He said, "Zacchaeus, come down immediately. I must stay at your house today."

Zacchaeus was glad when he heard this. He climbed down quickly and took Jesus to his house.

Some of the people in the crowd were displeased when they saw it. They thought it was wrong for Jesus to visit with a great sinner such as Zacchaeus, and they said so.

Jesus paid no attention to what the people said. He went with Zacchaeus to his house. To show how sorry he was for his sins, Zacchaeus said, "Look, Lord! Here and now I give half my possessions to the poor, and if I have cheated anybody out of anything, I will pay back four times the amount."

Jesus said to him, "Today salvation has come to this house, . . . For the Son of Man came to seek and to save what was lost."

The 10 Talents

Matthew 25:14–30

Jesus used the following parable to teach the people how He would have them use their time while they wait for His second coming.

When the word *talent* comes to mind, we usually think of some skill or ability a person may have. But in this parable it means a sum of money, about 2,000 dollars. This is the parable:

A certain rich man was about to go on a trip to a faraway country. Before he started on his way, he called three of his servants and put them in charge of his money. To each of the servants the master gave as many talents as he was able to use wisely. To the one he gave five, to the other two, and to the third just one. Then he went on his trip.

As soon as he was away, the servant with the five talents went to work with his money. By doing business with it, he earned another five talents. The second servant did equally well. With his two talents he earned another two. But the third servant, instead of using his one talent wisely, dug a hole and buried it.

After a long time the master returned from his trip. At once he had his three servants report to him on what they had done with his money. The first servant stepped forward, held out the money, and said, "Master, you entrusted me with five talents. See, I have gained five more."

The master was pleased, and he rewarded his servant immediately. "Well done, good and faithful servant!" he said. "You have been faithful with a few things; I will put you in charge of many things. Come and share your master's happiness!"

The second servant reported exactly as the first. He too had doubled the money his master gave him. Since he was as faithful as the first servant, he received an equal reward.

Finally the third servant made his report. Standing before his master with the talent he had received, he said, "I knew that you are a hard man, harvesting where you have not sown and gathering where you have not scattered seed. So I was afraid and went out and hid your talent in the ground. See, here is what belongs to you."

The master was not at all satisfied with what his servant had done. Angrily he said, "You wicked, lazy servant! So you knew that I harvest where I have not sown and gather where I have not scattered seed? Well then, you should have put my money on deposit with the bankers, so that when I returned I would have received it back with interest."

Turning to another servant, the master said, "Take the talent from him and give it to the one who has 10 talents. For everyone who has will be given more, and he will have an abundance. Whoever does not have, even what he has will be taken from him."

Then the master punished the unfaithful servant. "Throw that worthless servant outside, into the darkness, where there will be weeping and gnashing of teeth."

The master in the parable is Jesus. The servants are those who believe in Him. To each of them God has given certain talents, or skills and abilities. To some He has given more, to others less. But many or few, God wants us to be faithful in the use of them during our life here on earth. We are faithful when we use our talents to bring honor to the Savior, to build up His church, and to help our fellow human beings.

Jesus Anointed at Bethany

John 12:1–11

A few days before Jesus suffered and died, He went with His disciples to Bethany, where Lazarus, the man Jesus had raised from the dead, lived with his sisters, Mary and Martha.

Here a dinner was given in Jesus' honor. Martha served and Lazarus was sitting at the table with Jesus.

While they were eating, Mary went to Jesus with about a pint of very fine and costly perfume. She poured the perfume on Jesus' feet. Then she bent low and wiped His feet with her hair. She did this because she loved Jesus.

Judas was displeased when he saw what Mary had done. He asked, "Why wasn't this perfume sold and the money given to the poor? It was worth a year's wages."

Judas objected, not because he cared about the poor but because he was a thief. He was the one who kept the money bag for Jesus and His disciples, and he stole from it.

But Jesus was pleased with the thing Mary had done. He said, "Leave her alone. It was intended that she should save this perfume for the day of my burial. You will always have the poor among you, but you will not always have Me."

Meanwhile a large crowd came to see Jesus and Lazarus. Many put their faith in Jesus as their Savior.

Jesus Enters Jerusalem

Matthew 21:1–9

Jesus was on His way to Jerusalem. The time was near for Him to suffer and die to save the world from sin.

When Jesus came near a small town, He called two of His disciples and said, "Go to the village ahead of you, and at once you will find a donkey tied there, with her colt by her. Untie them and bring them to Me."

Jesus also said, "If anyone says anything to you, tell him that the Lord needs them, and he will send them right away."

The disciples went and found the animals. Everything happened as Jesus said it would, fulfilling the words of the prophet Zechariah, "Say to the Daughter of Zion, 'See, your king comes to you, gentle and riding on a donkey, on a colt, the foal of a donkey.' "

The disciples came back to Jesus and laid their coats on the colt to make a saddle. Next they set Jesus on the colt, and He began His ride to Jerusalem.

The people in Jerusalem heard that Jesus was coming, and large crowds came out to meet Him. Some of the people spread their coats on the road in front of Jesus. Others cut branches from palm trees and laid them on the road.

The crowds that went before Jesus and those that followed after Him praised Him joyfully. They shouted, "Hosanna to the Son of David! Blessed is He who comes in the name of the Lord! Hosanna in the highest!"

So Jesus rode into the city, the Savior and King who had come to Jerusalem to save His people from their sins.

The Widow's Offering

Luke 21:1–4

On one of His visits to the temple, Jesus sat down near the place where 13 offering boxes stood. Into these boxes the people put money for the upkeep of the temple.

For some time Jesus watched the people dropping money into the boxes. He saw rich people put large sums of money into them. He saw others give smaller sums.

While Jesus was sitting there watching, a poor widow passed by. She dropped two small copper coins, worth less than a penny, into one of the boxes.

Jesus was pleased with the offering of the poor widow. She was so thankful to God that she gave the last of her money. Calling His disciples, He said to them, "I tell you the truth, this poor widow has put in more than all the others. All these people gave their gifts out of their wealth; but she out of her poverty put in all she had to live on."

This widow had no money left for food and for the other things she needed. She depended on God, the heavenly Father, to give her food and clothing and whatever else she needed.

The 10 Virgins

Matthew 25:1–13

There will be a day when Jesus will come to earth for the second time. He will come as a mighty king, and He will judge all people. Because Jesus will judge everyone, we call the day of His second coming Judgment Day.

Jesus wanted to impress on His disciples how important it was to be ready for this day; therefore He told this parable about a wedding:

Ten young women were invited as bridesmaids to a wedding. Since the wedding was to take place at night, each of the girls took an oil lamp on the evening of the wedding day and went to the home of the bride. All of the girls wanted to meet the bridegroom when he came to get his bride and to go with him as he took her to his home for the wedding feast.

Now, five of the young women were foolish; they took no extra oil for their lamps. The other five were wise; they were thoughtful enough to take along bottles of extra oil, so they would be ready to meet the bridegroom, whether he came early or late.

The young women waited. Since the bridegroom delayed his coming, the girls became tired and fell asleep.

Suddenly at midnight they were awakened by a shout, "Here's the bridegroom! Come out to meet him!"

Immediately all the girls got up, prepared their lamps, and lighted them. But the foolish girls soon discovered that their oil was used up; so their lamps burned only a moment and then went out. But the wise young women, having extra oil, quickly refilled their lamps, so that they burned brightly.

The foolish girls, seeing the trouble they were in, frantically called to their wise friends for help. "Give us some of your oil," they pleaded, "our lamps are going out."

"No," the wise girls replied. "There may not be enough for both us and you. Instead go to those who sell oil and buy some some for yourselves."

Following this advice, the foolish girls hurried away. While the were trying to buy oil, the bridegroom arrived. The wise young women rushed to meet him. In great joy they went with him and his bride to his home for the wedding feast. When all were inside, the door was shut.

After a while the foolish girls returned. Standing in front of the closed door, they pleaded with the bridegroom, saying, "Sir, Sir, open the door for us!" But the bridegroom answered, "I tell you the truth, I don't know you."

Then Jesus, having finished the parable, added a word of warning for His disciples and for all of us. He said, "Therefore keep watch, because you do not know the day or the hour."

The bridegroom in the parable is Jesus. The bride is the church, or all the people who have received Jesus in faith as their Savior from sin. The wedding feast stands for the joys in heaven. The foolish young women represent all the people who once were believers, but who through neglect have allowed the light of their faith to go out. Thus they are pretenders, or Christians in name only. The wise young women are the true believers. Having been careful about the regular hearing and learning of God's Holy Word, the light of their faith is bright and strong. So they are ready at all times to meet Jesus with joy, knowing that they will be received into the glory of life with Him in heaven.

Jesus Teaches about the Judgment

Matthew 25:31–46

When the world comes to an end, Jesus will come in His glory and all the people that ever lived will stand before Him.

After Jesus separates them, He will say to those on His right, "Come, you who are blessed by My Father; take your inheritance, the kingdom prepared for you since the creation of the world. For I was hungry and you gave Me something to eat, I was thirsty and you gave Me something to drink, I was a stranger and you invited Me in, I needed clothes and you clothed Me, I was sick and you looked after Me, I was in prison and you came to visit Me."

Then those promised the kingdom of heaven will answer Jesus, "Lord, when did we see You hungry and feed You, or thirsty and give You something to drink? When did we see You a stranger and invite You in, or needing clothes and clothe You? When did we see You sick or in prison and go to visit You?"

Then Jesus will reply, "I tell you the truth, whatever you did for one of the least of these brothers of Mine, you did for Me."

Then Jesus will say to those on His left, "Depart from Me, you who are cursed, into the eternal fire prepared for the devil and his angels. For I was hungry and you gave Me nothing to eat, I was thirsty and you gave Me nothing to drink, I was a stranger and you did not invite Me in, I needed clothes and you did not clothe Me, I was sick and in prison and you did not look after Me."

The people on His left also will answer, "Lord, when did we see You hungry or thirsty or a stranger or needing clothes or sick or in prison, and did not help You?"

He will reply, "I tell you the truth, whatever you did not do for one of the least of these, you did not do for Me."

In these words Jesus taught that after those trusting in Him for salvation are separated from those without faith, He will judge all people. As children of God by faith we can look forward to this great day, knowing that Jesus has earned salvation for us. Meanwhile, the Holy Spirit moves us to respond to His goodness in the things we think, say, and do.

Jesus Washes the Disciples' Feet

John 13:1–17

It was just before the Passover Feast. Jesus knew that the time had come for Him to leave this world and go to His Father. Having loved His own who were in the world, He now showed them the full extent of His love.

The evening meal was being served, and the devil had already prompted Judas Iscariot, son of Simon, to betray Jesus. Jesus knew that the Father had put all things under His power, and that He had come from God and was returning to God; so He got up from the meal, took off His outer clothing, and wrapped a towel around His waist. After that, He poured water into a basin and began to wash His disciples' feet, drying them with the towel that was wrapped around Him.

He came to Simon Peter, who said to Him, "Lord, are you going to wash my feet?"

Jesus replied, "You do not realize now what I am doing, but later you will understand."

196

"No," said Peter, "You shall never wash my feet." By these words Peter wanted Jesus to know that he didn't consider himself worthy of having his Lord doing servant's work for him.

But Jesus answered, "Unless I wash you, you have no part with Me." Jesus wanted Peter and the disciples to know that unless they allowed Him to earn salvation for them, they could not be saved. About Jesus Matthew wrote, "The Son of Man did not come to be served, but to serve, and to give His life as a ransom for many."

Later when Jesus had finished washing the disciples' feet, He put on His outer clothes and, returning to His place, said, "Do you understand what I have done for you? You call Me 'Teacher' and 'Lord,' and rightly so, for that is what I am. Now that I, your Lord and Teacher, have washed your feet, you also should wash one another's feet."

By His actions Jesus gave His disciples an example to follow, promising His blessing upon the things they would do for others as a way of showing their love for Him.

The Last Supper

Matthew 26:14–30

After the devil had entered the heart of Judas, one of the 12 disciples of Jesus, and made Judas willing to betray Jesus, Judas went to the enemies of Jesus. He promised to help them capture Jesus if they would give him 30 pieces of silver. And from then on he watched for an opportunity to hand Jesus over to them.

Earlier on the day when Jesus washed the disciples' feet, they had asked Him where He wanted to eat the Passover meal.

Jesus said, "Go into the city to a certain man and tell him, 'The Teacher says: My appointed time is near. I am going to celebrate the Passover with My disciples at your house'." And the disciples did as Jesus had told them.

That evening, after Jesus had washed their feet, and they were gathered at the table about to have a last supper together, Jesus said, "I tell you the truth, one of you will betray Me."

The disciples were sad when they heard this, and one after another asked, "Surely not I, Lord?" Even Judas dared to ask.

Jesus answered Judas, "Yes, it is you."

As the rest were eating, Jesus took some bread, gave thanks to His heavenly Father, and broke it. Then He gave it to His disciples and said, "Take and eat; this is My body."

In the same way He took a cup of wine, and after giving thanks, He gave it to them, saying, "Drink from it, all of you. This is My blood of the covenant, which is poured out for many for the forgiveness of sins."

In these words Jesus gave to believers of all times a holy meal, to be celebrated often in His memory for the forgiveness, faith, and salvation Jesus promised as gifts to His people.

199

Judas Betrays Jesus

Matthew 26:30–56

On the night before Jesus died, after He and His disciples had celebrated the first Holy Communion, they sang a hymn and went together to the Mount of Olives. And Jesus told His disciples, "This very night you will all fall away on account of Me, for it is written, 'I will strike the shepherd, and the sheep of the flock will be scattered.' But after I have risen I will go ahead of you into Galilee."

But Peter said, "Even if all fall away on account of You, I never will."

"I tell you the truth," Jesus answered, "this very night, before the rooster crows, you will disown Me three times."

But Peter said even more strongly, "Even if I have to die with You, I will never disown You." All the other disciples said the same thing.

Then Jesus went with His disciples to a garden called Gethsemane. Leaving the rest of the disciples at a distance, Jesus took Peter, James, and John along with Him. Then asking them to watch and pray with Him, Jesus removed Himself from the three and prayed, "Father, if it is possible, may this cup be taken from Me. Yet not as I will, but as You will. My Father, if it is not possible for this cup to be taken away unless I drink it, may Your will be done."

By these words, Jesus asked His Father if there were another way to pay for the sins of the world other than to suffer a horrible and humiliating death for them.

Jesus prayed His prayer three times. In between He came back to check on His disciples. Each time He found them sleeping. Jesus realized that although they were willing to stay awake and pray, their bodies were tired. When He returned from praying the third time, He told the disciples to wake up. "Rise, let us go! Here comes My betrayer!"

While He was still speaking a crowd came up, and Judas was leading them. In those days, all friends greeted each other with a kiss.

Having planned in advance to let the group know which man was Jesus by kissing Him, Judas approached Jesus, said, "Greetings, Rabbi!" and kissed Him. But Jesus replied, "Friend, do what you came for."

When the men stepped forward to arrest Jesus, Peter pulled out his sword and swung it in Jesus' defense, cutting off the ear of the servant of the high priest.

But Jesus said, "Put your sword back in its place, for all who draw the sword will die by the sword. Do you think I cannot call on My Father, and He will at once put at My disposal more than 12 legions of angels? But how then would the Scriptures be fulfilled that say it must happen this way?"

Then Jesus said to the crowd, "Am I leading a rebellion, that you have come out with swords and clubs to capture Me? Every day I sat in the temple courts teaching, and you did not arrest Me. But this has all taken place that the writings of the prophets might be fulfilled."

Then all the disciples left Jesus. They all ran away.

Peter's Denial

Luke 22:54–62

After the crowd captured Jesus in Gethsemane, they brought Him to the house of the high priest. Peter followed at a distance.

The soldiers outside the high priest's house had built a fire in the courtyard to warm themselves, and Peter sat with them by the fire. Seeing Peter in the firelight, a servant girl looked closely at him and said, "This man was with Him."

But Peter denied it. "Woman, I don't know Him," he said.

A little while later someone else saw Peter and said, "You also are one of them."

"Man, I am not!" Peter shot back.

About an hour later someone else said about Peter, "Certainly this fellow was with Him, for he is a Galilean."

Peter's accent gave him away.

Growing ever more fearful, Peter replied, "Man I don't know what you're talking about!"

Just then two things happened. The rooster crowed and Jesus turned and looked straight at Peter. At this point Peter remembered Jesus' words, "Before the rooster crows today, you will disown Me three times."

Filled with sorrow and grief because of his sin, Peter rushed out of the courtyard and wept bitterly.

Jesus before Pilate and Herod

Luke 22:63–23:25; Matthew 27:1–5

After Jesus was arrested, the men guarding Him began to mock and beat Him. They insulted Him and after blindfolding Him demanded Him to prophesy which of them had hit Him.

At daybreak on Friday a council made up of the elders of the people, both the chief priests and teachers of the Law, met together. Jesus was brought before them. "If You are the Christ," they said, "tell us."

Jesus answered, "If I tell you, you will not believe Me . . . But from now on, the Son of Man will be seated at the right hand of the mighty God."

They all asked, "Are You then the Son of God?"

He replied, "You are right in saying I am."

At this the leaders were satisfied that Jesus' own words were enough to justify His being executed. According to Jewish law, blasphemy, or mocking God, was punishable by death. Jesus' claim to be God was *not* blasphemy. Jesus is the true and only Son of God.

Not being able on their own to carry out a death sentence, the leaders of the Jews brought Jesus to Pontius Pilate, the Roman governor.

When Judas realized that Jesus was going to die because he had handed Him over to the leaders of the people, he tried to undo his actions by returning the money he had been given for betraying his Lord. "I have sinned for I have betrayed innocent blood," he told the chief priests and elders. But they did not offer Judas any comfort or hope. "What is that to us?" they asked. "That's your responsibility." Then Judas threw the money into the temple and went out and hanged himself.

Knowing Pilate would think it foolish to put someone to death for claiming to be God, the chief priests and the elders accused Jesus as follows: "We have found this man subverting our nation. He opposes payment of taxes to Caesar and claims to be Christ, a king."

So Pilate asked Jesus, "Are You the king of the Jews?"

"Yes, it is as you say," Jesus replied.

But Pilate said, "I find no basis for a charge against this man."

But the crowd insisted, "He stirs up the people all over Judea by His teaching. He started in Galilee and has come all the way here."

When Pilate learned that Jesus was a Galilean he sent Jesus to Herod, the ruler of Galilee, who was visiting in Jerusalem at that time.

Herod was happy to see Jesus because he had heard about Him, and he hoped to see Him do some miracle. Herod asked Jesus many questions, but Jesus gave Him no answer. In the presence of Herod, the chief priests and the teachers of the Law accused Jesus. Then Herod and his soldiers ridiculed and mocked Him. They put an elegant robe on Jesus and sent Him back to Pilate.

Pilate told the accusers of Jesus that neither he nor Herod had found any basis for the charge that Jesus was working to start a rebellion against the Roman government. Pilate hoped to get the people to recognize that Jesus had done nothing deserving of death. Because it was a custom for the governor to release a prisoner during the celebration of the Passover, Pilate planned to punish Jesus, in order to satisfy the people, and then let Him go.

But when the people learned of Pilate's plan they shouted together, "Away with this man! Release Barabbas to us!"

Now Barabbas was a criminal who had been arrested for stirring up trouble in the city, and for murder.

Wanting to release Jesus, Pilate spoke to the crowd again and again, hoping to appeal to their sense of justice. But they kept shouting, "Crucify Him! Crucify Him!"

Finally Pilate gave in. He set Barabbas free and handed Jesus, an innocent man, over to the people to be put to death in a cruel and horrible manner, suspended between heaven and earth on a wooden cross.

Jesus' Death and Burial

Matthew 27:33–44; Mark 15:22–32; Luke 23:26–56; John 19:17–24

Outside the city of Jerusalem was a place called Calvary, where Jesus' crucifixion was to take place. Jesus was led there by the soldiers. Jesus carried His cross part of the way. Then the soldiers made a man named Simon carry it the rest of the way. Some people cried for Jesus. They did not know that Jesus was suffering and dying for them.

The enemies of Jesus crucified Him. They nailed His hands and feet to the cross. Jesus' cross was put up between two others, on which robbers were crucified. Soldiers took Jesus' clothes. His enemies called Him names and mocked Him. Even the robbers on the cross mocked Him.

This added to Jesus' suffering. For about six hours Jesus hung on the cross, giving up His life in a most painful way in order to pay for the sins of the whole world.

Jesus spoke seven times from the cross. These words tell us how He felt and what was happening.

First Jesus prayed for His enemies who put Him on the cross. He said, "Father, forgive them, for they do not know what they are doing."

Then one of the robbers was sorry for his sins and prayed to Jesus. He said, "Jesus, remember me when You come into Your kingdom."

Jesus said to him, "I tell you the truth, today you will be with Me in paradise."

Jesus looked down from the cross and saw His mother, Mary, and His disciple John. He said to Mary, "Dear woman, here is your son." To John He said, "Here is your mother!" From that time John took care of Mary in his own house.

Then Jesus said, "I am thirsty." His enemies gave Him vinegar to drink.

As Jesus suffered on the cross, darkness came over the land. Jesus cried, "My God, My God, why have You forsaken Me?"

Soon after that Jesus knew that His work was done. He had paid the price of sin.

From noon to three o'clock it was dark over the whole land. Then Jesus shouted in victory, "It is finished!" His last words were, "Father, into Your hands I commit My spirit."

Then He bowed His head and died. At that moment the curtain of the temple tore in two, from top to bottom, an earthquake shook the land, and tombs broke open as many holy people who had died were raised to life. Seeing this a Roman centurion praised God saying, "Surely this was a righteous man."

Late in the afternoon some of Jesus' friends asked Pilate for the body of the Lord. They took down the body and laid it in a grave.

They closed the door of the grave with a large stone. Some women who loved Jesus watched as they buried Him.

The Resurrection

Matthew 28:1–15; Luke 24:1–31; John 20:1–18

It was the Sunday morning after Jesus had died on the cross. Soldiers were guarding the grave when suddenly the earth shook and a great light shone down from heaven.

An angel came and rolled away the stone from the door of the grave. The soldiers became afraid. They fell to the ground as if they were dead.

The grave was empty! Jesus was alive again! The soldiers got up and ran into the city. They told Jesus' enemies everything that had happened.

Then the enemies gave money to the soldiers. They told them to say that they had been sleeping and that the disciples had taken the body of Jesus away.

Very early the same morning some of the women who believed in Jesus came out to the grave. They saw that the grave was open. What had happened? Jesus was not there.

Then the angel gave them this message: "Do not be afraid, for I know that you are looking for Jesus, who was crucified. He is not here; He has risen, just as He said. Come and see the place where He lay. Then go quickly and tell His disciples, 'He has risen from the dead and is going ahead of you into Galilee. There you will see Him.' Now I have told you."

At once the women hurried to bring the message to the disciples.

That same morning Jesus showed Himself alive first to Mary Magdalene. Mary was crying when Jesus suddenly stood near her and spoke to her. Mary thought the man in charge of the garden was speaking.

"Sir," she said, "if you have carried Him away, tell me where you have put Him and I will get Him."

"Mary!" said Jesus.

Now Mary knew Jesus. She cried, "Rabboni!" (which means teacher).

Jesus asked Mary to tell His disciples that He was alive again and that soon He would go to His Father in heaven.

Mary was very happy on that Easter Day. She ran to the disciples and gave them the message that Jesus was alive.

On the afternoon of the first Easter Day, two disciples left Jerusalem to walk to the little town of Emmaus. As they walked they talked together of all the things that had happened to Jesus.

A stranger joined them and listened. It was Jesus Himself. But Jesus did not want the disciples to know Him at once, and so they did not know Him.

Jesus said, "What are you discussing together as you walk along?"

The disciples answered, "Are you only a visitor to Jerusalem that you do not know the things that have happened there in these days?"

"What things?" Jesus asked.

They began to tell Him how the enemies of Jesus had put Him to death on the cross. They said, "We had hoped He was the one who was going to redeem Israel. And what is more, it is the third day since all this took place. In addition, some of our women amazed us. They went to the tomb early this morning but didn't find His body. They came and told us that they had seen a vision of angels who said He was alive. Then some of our companions went to the tomb and found it just as the women had said, but Him they did not see."

"How foolish you are," said the stranger. "And how slow of heart to believe all that the prophets have spoken! Did not Christ have to suffer these things and then enter His glory?"

Then the stranger explained to them all the sayings in the Scriptures that showed that Jesus had to suffer and die to be the Savior. The disciples listened. How happy they were that this stranger helped them understand God's Word!

When they came to the village, the stranger acted as though He would go farther. But the disciples did not want Him to leave them. They said, "Stay with us, for it is nearly evening; the day is almost over."

The stranger was willing to stay with them. As they sat down to eat, He took bread and prayed and gave it to them.

Suddenly the disciples' eyes were opened, and they knew it was Jesus. As soon as they knew Him, Jesus was gone.

Doubting Thomas

Luke 24:36–48; John 20:24–30

On the evening of Easter Sunday the disciples of Jesus were gathered together in a room. They locked all the doors, for they were afraid of the enemies of Jesus who had crucified their Lord. All of the disciples were there except Thomas.

Suddenly Jesus stood among them. "Peace be with you!" He said.

At first the disciples were not sure that it was Jesus. They thought they saw a spirit. They were afraid.

Then Jesus said, "Why are you troubled, and why do doubts rise in your minds? Look at My hands and My feet. It is I Myself! Touch Me and see; a ghost does not have flesh and bones, as you see I have."

Jesus showed His disciples His hands and feet.

While they wondered, Jesus said, "Do you have anything here to eat?"

They gave Him some broiled fish and Jesus ate it. Then the disciples knew that this was really their Lord who was crucified and had become alive again. Jesus talked to them for a while, and then He was gone.

When Thomas returned, the other disciples told him, "We have seen the Lord!" But Thomas would not believe them. He said, "Unless I see the nail marks in His hands and put my finger where the nails were, and put my hand into His side, I will not believe it."

A week later the disciples were together again. This time Thomas was with them. Though the doors were locked, suddenly Jesus came and stood among them in the room. "Peace be with you," He said.

Then Jesus turned to Thomas. "Put your finger here; see My hands. Reach out your hand and put it into My side. Stop doubting and believe."

Now Thomas believed that Jesus had risen from the dead and was really alive. He said, "My Lord and my God!" Then Jesus told him, "Because you have seen Me, you have believed; blessed are those who have not seen and yet have believed."

Jesus and the Miraculous Catch of Fish

John 21:1–17

One day Simon Peter and John and five other disciples were together at the Sea of Galilee. "I'm going out to fish," said Peter.

"We'll go with you," they answered.

So they rowed their boat out on the sea and fished all night, but they did not catch anything.

Early the next morning Jesus stood on the shore, but the disciples did not know it was Jesus. He called to them and asked whether they had caught anything.

They answered, "No." He said to them, "Throw your nets on the right side of the boat and you will find some." They obeyed, and soon they were not able to pull up the net because there were so many fish in it.

John knew now who the man on the shore was. "It is the Lord," he said. When Simon Peter heard that it was the Lord, he put on his coat and jumped into the water to wade to the shore. The other disciples came in the boat, dragging the net with fish.

As soon as they had come to land, they saw a fire there, and fish laid on it, and bread. Jesus said to them, "Come and have breakfast."

After the disciples had eaten, Jesus said to Simon Peter, "Simon son of John, do you truly love Me more than these?"

Peter answered, "Yes, Lord, You know that I love You."

Jesus said to him, "Feed My lambs."

Again Jesus said, "Simon son of John, do you truly love Me?"

Peter answered, "Yes, Lord, You know that I love You."

Jesus said, "Take care of My sheep."

Then, for the third time, Jesus asked, "Simon son of John, do you truly love Me?"

Now Peter was sad because Jesus had asked him this question the third time. He remembered how he had three times denied Jesus in the house of the high priest. He was truly sorry for that, and therefore he said, "Lord, You know all things; You know that I love You."

Jesus said to him, "Feed My sheep."

Jesus had fully forgiven Peter's sin, and Peter was now to teach both the little children and grown people about Jesus the Savior.

The Ascension

Luke 24:50–53; Acts 1:1–11

On the 40th day after Easter the disciples of Jesus were again together in Jerusalem, and Jesus was with them. It was near the time for Jesus to go to heaven, and He had many things to say to the disciples. Especially did He speak about the wonderful things that had happened in the past few weeks—things which had been foretold about Him in the Scriptures.

Jesus helped them understand the Scriptures. He reminded them about the Savior having to suffer and die and then rise again from the dead the third day, and that the good news of forgiveness should be told to all people.

Then Jesus commanded them not to leave Jerusalem, but to wait for the gift of the Holy Spirit. He said, "You will receive power when the Holy Spirit comes on you, and you will be My witnesses in Jerusalem, and in all Judea and Samaria, and to the ends of the earth."

Then standing on the Mount of Olives, Jesus lifted up His hands and blessed His disciples. While He blessed them, He was taken from them and carried up into heaven.

When the disciples looked toward heaven as He went up, two men suddenly stood by them, clothed in white. They said, "Men of Galilee, why do you stand here looking into the sky? This same Jesus, who has been taken from you into heaven, will come back in the same way."

The disciples now returned to Jerusalem with great joy and worshiped in the temple, praising God.

G. MYERS

The First Pentecost

Acts 2:1–41

Pentecost was a great holy day of the people. It was kept 50 days after the Passover. Many would come together in Jerusalem for this holy day. On this day the disciples were all together in one place.

Suddenly a sound like a rushing, mighty wind was heard. The Holy Spirit came to the disciples, and soon one could see little tongues like fire on each one of the disciples as a sign that the Holy Spirit had been sent to them.

Another miracle was that every disciple could speak in languages which he had never learned before. Soon the people began to hear of these wonderful things. They hurried to see the disciples and to hear what they had to say.

Peter now stood up and began to speak to the people. He told them that what was happening was the work of the Holy Spirit. He told them that God had sent His Son, Jesus, to be the Savior of the world, but that they had crucified Him. On the third day, however, He had risen from the dead and was now alive.

Many of the people, when they heard Peter's words, were troubled and afraid because of their sins. They asked the disciples, "Brothers, what shall we do?"

Peter said, "Repent and be baptized, every one of you, in the name of Jesus Christ for the forgiveness of your sins and you will receive the gift of the Holy Spirit. The promise is for you and your children and for all who are far off—for all whom the Lord our God will call."

By these words Peter told of God's saving love for people of all times and places, including people living today—many years after the first Pentecost.

But this day marked the beginning of the Christian church.

More than 3,000 people who heard Peter's sermon believed in Jesus and received forgiveness of sins.

This was the work of the Holy Spirit—the same Holy Spirit who is now at work all over the world wherever the good news of Jesus, the Savior, is told.

The Conversion of Paul

Acts 9:1–22

One of the greatest enemies of the young Christian church was a man whose name was Saul. At one time he went from house to house and arrested Christians and put them into prison.

One day he went to the high priest in Jerusalem. Saul asked for letters that would introduce him to the synagogue leaders in Damascus. He wanted to arrest Christians in Damascus, too, and bring them bound to Jerusalem.

The high priest gave Saul the letters, and Saul, together with some other men, went to Damascus.

As Saul and his men came to Damascus, suddenly a light from heaven shone around him. Saul and his men fell to the ground.

Then Saul heard a voice saying to him, "Saul, Saul, why do you persecute Me?"

Saul said, "Who are You, Lord?"

The voice answered, "I am Jesus, whom you are persecuting. Now get up and go into the city, and you will be told what you must do."

Saul arose from the ground and opened his eyes, but he could not see! The other men had to lead him by the hand.

They brought him to Damascus, to the house of a friend whose name was Judas. There he stayed for three days without being able to see. Nor did he eat or drink anything.

In Damascus there lived a Christian whose name was Ananias. The Lord appeared to him and said, "Go to the house of Judas on Straight Street and ask for a man from Tarsus named Saul, for he is praying."

Ananias answered, "Lord, I have heard many reports about this man and all the harm he has done to Your saints in Jerusalem. And he has come here with authority from the chief priests to arrest all who call on Your name."

But the Lord said, "Go! This man is My chosen instrument to carry My name before the Gentiles and their kings and before the people of Israel." So Ananias went.

Ananias found Saul and he laid his hands on him and said, "Brother Saul, the Lord—Jesus, who appeared to you on the road as you were coming here—has sent me so that you may see again and be filled with the Holy Spirit."

All at once Saul could see again, and he arose and was baptized. No longer did he want to hurt the Christians, for now he was a Christian himself.

From that time on he used his other name—Paul—and became a great missionary for Jesus. He traveled to many faraway places to tell sinners about Jesus, the Savior.

The Adventures of Paul

1 Timothy 1:12–17; 2 Corinthians 11:24–12:10; Romans 11:33–36a

After God changed Paul's life, he became a brand new person. Once a blasphemer, a persecutor, and a violent man, Paul became a Christian when God gave him the gift of faith in Christ Jesus.

Paul thanked God for the great change that came into his life. He delighted in the abundant grace, love, and patience of a God who would call sinners to be His servants.

As God the Spirit enabled him, Paul boldly told the Good News of the salvation available to all who trust in Christ Jesus—including the very worst of sinners, as Paul considered himself to be.

And Paul's work of sharing the Gospel was not easy. At first other Christians were afraid of him. And why shouldn't they be. Paul was the man who used to work tirelessly to wipe them out. Only a mighty and wonderful God could change a person so drastically.

But God's power didn't stop when Saul/Paul became a Christian. In Paul's missionary journeys God helped Paul to work hard and to endure prison, beatings, and the threat of death time and again in order to bring the Gospel of forgiveness, life, and eternal happiness to those who did not know Jesus as their Savior.

Throughout his life and work, the Savior who came to Saul/Paul on the road to Damascus never left him. Once when Paul's enemies were looking to arrest him, Jesus protected Paul and allowed him to escape the city by being lowered in a basket from a window in the city wall.

Later in his ministry Paul recalled his adventures. He said, "Five times I received from the Jews the forty lashes minus one. Three times I was beaten with rods, once I was stoned, three times I was shipwrecked, I spent a night and a day in the open sea, I have been constanly on the move. I have been in danger from rivers, in danger from bandits, in danger from my own countrymen, in danger from Gentiles; in danger in the city, in danger in the country, in danger at sea; and in danger from false

223

brothers. I have labored and toiled and have often gone without sleep; I have known hunger and thirst and have often gone without food; I have been cold and naked."

In his life and ministry God taught Paul an important lesson. Paul learned that he could be happy in all times—both good and bad—because Jesus was always faithful to His promises. He always remained with Paul, offering him peace, joy, and strength, even when things weren't going very well for him.

And God's love for Paul is the same as His love for us. Because Jesus is our Savior we need never feel sad, lonely, or useless. Just as He did for Paul, Jesus will go with us, wherever we go. He will never leave us. Just as He did for Paul, God will provide us with many people with whom we can share the good news of Jesus' life, death, and resurrection so that they too may come to believe in Him. What a great God and Savior we have! How wonderfully He provides for His people.

In the following words of Paul He is praised, "Oh, the depths of the riches of wisdom and knowledge of God! How unsearchable His judgments, and His paths beyond tracing out!"

" 'Who has known the mind of the Lord? Or who has been His counselor?' "

" 'Who has ever given to God, that God should repay him?' For from Him and through Him and to Him are all things . . . "

"Now to the King, eternal, immortal, invisible, the only God, be honor and glory for ever and ever. Amen."